The Christian
Philosophy of Science

The Christian Philosophy of Science

Herman Bavinck

Translated by: Jan Adriaan Schlebusch

RefCon Press

The Christian Philosophy of Science

Copyright © 2022
Published by **RefCon Press**
      7901 4th St. North Ste. #8193
      St. Petersburg, FL 33702

RefCon Press is the publishing imprint of:
The Reformed Conservative
www.thereformedconservative.org
admin@thereformedconservative.org

Originally published in Dutch by Herman Bavinck as *Christelijke Wetenschap*, by J.H. Kok (Kampen) in 1904. The Dutch version of this work is in the public domain.

Library of Congress Control Number: 2022937770

ISBN: 978-1-954504-03-5
eBook ISBN: 978-1-954504-02-8

Translator: Jan Adriaan Schlebusch
General Editor: Robert J. McPherson II

To the Reformed Conservatives

Defend. Strengthen. Build.

Contents

Translator's Preface

In 1904, at the height of his career, the influential Dutch Neo-Calvinist theologian Herman Bavinck published this book on the Christian Philosophy of Science under its original Dutch title *Christelijke Wetenschap*. Within Bavinck's corpus, this book occupies a unique position by virtue of its focus. Bavinck is best known as a systematic theologian, but he produced this publication as well as his book *Christian Worldview* in 1904 at a time when he evidently felt pressed to contribute to a holistic Christian philosophy. The latter work was first translated into English in 2019 by Cory C. Brock, James Eglinton, and Nathaniel Gray Sutanto, and published by Crossway Books—a testimony to the growing interest both in the Anglosphere and around the world in Bavinck's philosophical works.

Herman Bavinck's book, *The Christian Philosophy of Science*, needs to be viewed in the context of what he describes as a reawakening of the desire to reengage in the field of science within the framework of

Christian principles in the Netherlands at the turn of the twentieth century. Bavinck voices the concerns of many Christian scientists and scholars at the time who had already become disillusioned with the methodological positivism prevalent in the field of science during most of the nineteenth century. In this regard, Bavinck was well ahead of his time, since he wrote this book almost 60 years before positivism would be widely discarded in academic scholarship throughout the West.

Bavinck counters modern science's endless search for causes by arguing that any scientific investigation whatsoever presupposes a faith in the existence of a rational order and consistent logic operating in creation. He further contends that such order and logic can only be the work of a Sovereign Creator. He, therefore, defines science itself as the interpretation of divine thought as it manifests in divine works. True science should always lead to increased knowledge of and reverence for God. He argues that the Christian philosophy of science is furthermore unmissable for scientific scholarship given the reality of human nature itself. Since human beings are depraved, humans have a tendency to distort truth for the sake of self-interest and only the self-evaluation demanded by the gospel of Jesus Christ can keep us on the path to finding scientific truth. For Bavinck, true science is necessarily Christocentric, since it is only through Jesus Christ that all objects of scientific study find meaning and purpose.

In our contemporary context, the Christian philosophy of science has become an increasingly pressing matter given the increasing impact the scientific community has had on our lives during and after the COVID-19 pandemic. Debates regarding virology, immunology, and medical mandates have profound ethical, political, and theological implications. The leftist Green Agenda based on a theory of climate change that is fundamentally incompatible with Scripture should be a pressing matter for the Church. The time when many Christians limited their scientific engagement to debating evolution theory has long passed. The need for a comprehensive Christian philosophy of science as a framework for engaging in medical and environmental issues is now as pressing as it has ever been. While much work still needs to be done in this regard, I believe that this translation of Bavinck's most comprehensive work on this topic can be fruitful in terms of constructively directing future work done toward this end.

Jan Adriaan Schlebusch

Introduction

Over the past few years, we have witnessed the powerful and serious reawakening of the desire to restructure science in accordance with the Christian faith. Others can disagree with the value of such a desire, but its existence is beyond any doubt. The share of people disillusioned by the direction of the currently prevalent philosophy of science—both in terms of its theory and its practice—increases by the day. Many now desire a different principle for scientific scholarship and a different method of scientific investigation.

With regard to the origin and nature of this desire, there can also be no doubt. It is clear for all those with eyes to see that this desire proceeds from and is driven by religious motives. It is for the sake of religion, in the interest of the Christian faith, for the sake of overcoming the divide between theory and practice, and in defense of the confession of the Church that contemporary scientific investigation is condemned in terms of both its principles and method. Even the adherents of contemporary science cannot remain blind to the religious character of this movement. Only a short while ago, Professor Groenewegen at the University of Leiden appropriately remarked: "As the religious reaction quietly proceeded, the ecclesiastical and political reaction followed. Scientists are to recognize this reality, as well as the religious motives behind it, which provides it with a most honorable character."

And it is indeed honorable. After Christians had, in the eighteenth century, gradually sunk into a deep sleep, there was a sudden reawakening at the start of the nineteenth, which awakened the Christian, confessional and ecclesiastical consciousness from its slumber. And, as they suddenly noticed all around them how much had already been neglected and abandoned, the believers again started laboring for the Kingdom of God. The movement known as the *Réveil,* in particular, dedicated itself to evangelistic and philanthropic endeavors. The split in the Dutch Reformed Church back in 1834 also reformed the Church and restored her to her confessional foundations. In the political sphere, there was a great battle for the establishment and recognition of Christian schools. And so gradually it was realized that even in the sphere of science it had once again become necessary to hold up the banner of the gospel. Despite suffering much maltreatment and defamation, the theologian Jan Jacob Van Oosterzee defended a distinctly Christian view of science.

Likewise, Chantepie de la Saussaye bravely opposed empiricism. And ever since believers have, in the battle against science based in unbelief, taken an increasingly principled stance. The Theological University of Kampen, under orders from the Reformed Churches, has increasingly emphasized the need of a scientific education for future ministers of the Word, for the purpose of preparing them for the ministry. The Free University of Amsterdam has made it its purpose to teach all science in accordance with Reformed principles. We have, in fact, made so many inroads here in the Netherlands that a bill regarding the establishment of chairs in the sciences reserved for Christian professors has already been accepted by 56 votes to 41 in parliament. Even if only to a limited degree, the revival of the Christian philosophy of science is already evident, which should in itself fill our hearts with a joyous hope for the future.

This phenomenon in our fatherland is all the more remarkable and meaningful because it is in no way an isolated one. The signs of similar scientific movements are also evident elsewhere. Among the Roman Catholic Christians, especially after the publication of Pope Leo XIII's Encyclical in August 1879, in which he recommends a renewed appreciation of Aquinas, a revitalized zeal for scientific investigation in accordance with their principles emerged—one which should put Protestants to shame. There is literally no field of science in which they do not now have competent representatives. Through principled scholarship and precise scientific investigation, Roman Catholic principles are consistently applied in the sciences. Logic and psychology, metaphysics and theology, history and literature, jurisprudence and sociology are all so thoroughly practiced by Catholics, that it is something to be reckoned with by any and all opposition. And while the antithesis between us and them—something upon which the recent work of Denifle on Luther has cast renewed light—can in no way be trivialized, their scientific contributions can be fruitfully consulted by everyone who wishes to stand upon the foundation of an undoubted Christian faith.

But we can go further and view this revival of Christian scientific investigation in relation to a whole series of phenomena, which all point to the fact that the days of positivism are numbered. The motto "Back to Kant" has lost much of its appeal. The affinity for the philosophies of Hume and Comte is increasingly being replaced by an affinity for Leibniz and Hegel. Everywhere a return from empiricism to idealism can be seen. The idea of the sovereignty of the mind is being replaced by a devotion to the senses; theory is giving way to practice and rationalism to romanticism. In the arts, mysticism is making a comeback. Even in science, we are witnessing a development that was completely unthinkable just ten years ago, when materialism was held to be the highest truth and mechanical interpretation the only scientific theory of causality. Nowadays we bear witness to the fact that many of the world's leading scientists are turning away from mechanism to dynamism, from materialism to energetics, from the causal to the teleological, and from atheism to theism. After the initial thirst for facts has been quenched, a hunger for the knowledge of their origin and purpose—of the ultimate First Cause and essence of reality—emerges.

This remarkable turnaround in the sciences is also to be credited to our theological endeavors. It was not long ago that many scientists, historians, and philosophers doubted theology's very right to exist as an academic field. Just a few years ago, Haeckel believed that with the publication of his *Welträthsel,* he had dealt the death blow to theology and brought an end to the doctrines of God, the soul, and immortality. But the unenthusiastic reception of his work in academic circles proved that the general trend had already proceeded in a wholly different direction. The need and desire for the metaphysical are too deeply implanted in human nature to simply smother it. Moreover, the satisfaction provided by so many by means of spiritism and theosophy, humanism and cultural idolization, Buddhism and Islam all point to the inevitability of religion.

A widespread desire for a return to the Christian faith can also now be seen throughout all spheres of society. People have grown tired of uncertainty and doubt. Even among many liberal theologians, the desire for a confessional faith, for dogma, for ecclesiastical organization, and for a traditional liturgy has exhibited itself. The faith in an anthropocentric modern culture has been shaken. The hard sciences have not delivered that which the likes of a youthful Renan had expected of it. And so many people, even if not through genuine repentance but through dispirited doubt, now return to that formerly defamed religion.

A time such as this—one which is characterized by such trends—can by no means be unfavorable to scientific endeavors based upon Christian principles. For this very reason, it is so important that all of us, and all our friends and foes, become acquainted with what exactly is entailed by such scientific endeavors, which cannot simply and wrongly be reduced to reactionary dogmatism. All those who realize the power and strength of religious conviction, the impetus of principles, the roots of life itself, along with all those who recognize the signs of the times, cannot make themselves guilty of underestimating its power and influence, nor stand indifferent towards it. The faithful and faithless—or Christian and positivistic—conceptions of science stand in direct contradiction to one another. A choice between the two is inevitable, for which an understanding of the unique characteristics of each is vital.

How The Concept Of A Christian Philosophy Of Science Came To Be

For eighteen centuries, Christianity had been proclaimed in accordance with the doctrines of the apostles on this continent, which resulted in Europe being not only a mighty force but also a well-ordered society with a sophisticated culture. Yet, the signs of apostasy and decline had already been present 150 years ago. The golden age that science had experienced before the middle of the eighteenth century had passed, and its creativity had been exhausted. Eclectic and syncretic thinkers sought to preserve what they valued in existing systems. Mysticism sought to find a new path to knowledge through meditation and asceticism. And Skepticism sneeringly begged the question: What is truth?

Back in the first century, in a world characterized by unbelief and superstition, the apostles of Jesus planted the banner of truth. The Christian religion is, after all, not only the religion of grace but also the religion of truth. She is the one precisely because she is also the other. It is for this reason that Holy Scripture so often addresses the issue of truth: its essence and value are highlighted throughout all of Revelation. God Himself is truth, in contradistinction to all creations, in particular humans, who are not only mendacious but are, along with the idols, insignificant and vain. Because absolute truth is found in God alone, and because He alone is light without darkness, therefore all that comes from Him—His words and works, His ways and His commandments— are necessarily always truthful. Everything He does rests firmly upon truth and right as the immovable pillars of His works.

Christ Himself, as the Way, the Truth, and the Life, is the highest and most complete revelation of God. He is the Word who was in the beginning with God and was Himself, God. He is the image of the unseeable God, the imprint of His glory and independence, in whom the fullness of divinity dwells and in whom all the treasures of wisdom and knowledge can be found. What no one could achieve, He has done. No one has ever seen God; the only Son, who is at the Father's side, has made Him known. He has revealed His name to us, along with the knowledge of His truth. Christ persevered in this revelation of the name of His Father even unto death; under Pontius Pilate, He confessed the divine truth;

He is the trustworthy Witness, the Firstborn of the dead. His gospel is also the Word of truth. And in order that we believe and understand this gospel, He has sent us His Holy Spirit, whom, as the Spirit of Truth, leads us in all truth and seals it in our hearts. Whosoever accepts this gospel in faith has embraced the truth and has been regenerated, sanctified, and liberated by the truth. They are in the truth and the truth is in them. They speak and act in accordance with the truth and are willing to lay down their lives for it.

Powerful was the impact of this gospel of truth upon the Gentile nations. In a society undermined by doubt and unbelief, the apostles and after them crowds of men and women acted, driven by the conviction of a single, absolute, and infallible truth, acquirable by faith, and one which gifts life, liberty, and salvation to all who accept it in obedience to God. This wonder cannot be sufficiently expressed with words. Its impact upon man is as if we have been drowning at sea, and once again feel solid ground beneath our feet after having been rescued. Doubt made room for certainty, fear for trust, and anxiety for unprecedented joy.

The writings of the first Christians copiously bear witness to this fact. Therein they expressed their sincere conviction that in the gospel of Christ, they possessed the truth—a treasure that made them richer than all the scholars of their age. Because the world with all its wisdom had not known Christ, it pleased

God to, through the foolishness of the preaching of the gospel, redeem all who believe. God ordained that the wisdom of the wise should perish and that the knowledge of the knowledgeable should be destroyed. The wisdom of the world was revealed to be nothing more than foolishness and vain philosophies, but the gospel revealed itself as and proved itself to be the power and wisdom of God. This the Apostle Paul proclaimed when he wrote that every thought of the mind and desire of the heart ought to be taken captive in obedience to Christ, and so all the faithful after him have proclaimed as well. Christianity is the true philosophy, and Christians are the true philosophers, who know the truth and know the true God, and, by virtue of this knowledge, gain a better insight into the essence of creation, including that of nature and history. A highly developed self-consciousness in this regard was characteristic of the early Church. They were the people of God, the oldest people on earth, for whose sake the world had been created, and who now, in the New Covenant, reconciled all the opposition between Jew and Greek and heathen in a higher unity, and who had not only been called to a task of cosmic significance, but whom with Christ had become the true heirs of all things.

With this conviction, the first Christians formed an independent community, with their own lifestyle, with a unique worldview. Antithetically they stood against the world and had little in common with it. They fought idolatry and the worship of images, demonism and witchcraft, the idolization of man and of the emperor, as well as the theatres and the plays. They opposed all the prevailing popular notions and the lifestyle and aspirations of the time. But they could not simply remain content with this antithesis. The Apostle Paul had already shown that the faithful, if they were to break ties with the unbelievers, had to separate themselves from the world. But the impossibility thereof was realized more and more. This became all the more evident when not only slaves, but also masters, tradesmen, government officials, artists, and philosophers became Christians. The practice of separation was not viable anymore, and the need for a positive arrangement had become evident.

Even in the field of science, this same need arose. And here it was particularly difficult to find the right way amid the maze of different systems and schools. It is little wonder that so many lost their way and descended from the true path. The North African School, represented by Tertullian, stood on the one side, arguing that pagan works offer no value for Christianity since they have been revealed as nothing more than foolishness in the sight of God. He argued that philosophy is a vain, worldly endeavor, which cannot teach Christians anything, much less be practiced by them. What do Athens and Jerusalem, the academy and the Church, or the heretics and the Christians have in common? We are in no need of philosophy since Christ has brought us the true gospel. As long as we believe, we are in need of nothing else.

Over against the North African School stood the Alexandrian School, with their teachers Clement and Origen. They regarded faith as inferior to science and therefore strove to elevate faith itself to the level of "true knowledge" in order to make it more complete. Just as the development from Paganism to Christianity had been the first great improvement, so the development from Christianity to knowledge would be the second. This is because they believed that faith is based in fear, but knowledge is based in love, and serves as the affirmation of what is believed. In order to then help faith transition into knowledge, pagan science as the fruit of the Logos was held in such high esteem that the Christian truth was by means of allegorical explanations so generalized that it could actually be harmonized with pagan wisdom. And so, a typical mediating theology was created, which not only sought to tear down the antithesis between the divine truth and man-made science but ended up doing an injustice to both.

Yet both these positions have had their share of representatives and spokesmen throughout the history of the Church. At all times there have been those who have leaned over to one side or the other—either serving the world or escaping from it, idolizing the culture or despising culture, *Aufklärung* or pietism, rationalism or mysticism have been embraced by many throughout history. But neither of these tendencies can be reconciled to Christian truth. Therefore, the claim by Edwin Hatch and Adolf Harnack, namely that Christian theology is a marriage between the original gospel and Greek philosophy, is untenable. Undoubtedly, classical philosophy was utilized in service of the gospel, and the development of theology, if measured by Reformed standards, was for a very long time by no means error-free. But recognizing this by no means entails that the doctrine of the Church was the result of the outworking of Greek philosophy upon the gospel.

After all, Christian theologians, warned by the one-sidedness of the North African and Alexandrian schools, have long consciously and clearly set out the position of Christian truth over against pagan science. They came to the realization, however, that this is neither to be altogether rejected nor accepted. According to Paul, all things had to be tried and tested, but only that which had revealed itself to be good maintained. Therefore, the figurines which the people of God took with them from Egypt were dearly loved, and Solomon could also build his temple with the help of Hiram's servants and the cedars of Lebanon.

It would be Augustine who would eventually show Christians the most appropriate way and draw up the foundations of a true Christian philosophy of science. From his youth, he had been driven by a burning love of truth. He would not be content, as Lessing would be later, with the mere quest for truth; he longed for truth itself. After searching for this in vain with the Manicheans, with the Sceptics, with Plato and Plotinus, he finally found it in the Church with the gospel of Jesus Christ. From then on, he contrasted two potential sources of truth with one another: authority and reason. Philosophy in itself is insufficient to reveal to us the truth because human reason is limited by virtue of being depraved by sin. Its pride and egocentric nature stand in its own way. Science can therefore only teach us partial truths partially. It knows not the path that leads to truth because it does not know Christ, and therefore often results in mere labyrinths. God has provided us with another authoritative epistemic source. Because we are preoccupied with that which is earthly and naturally reject that which is eternal, faith is necessary, as a "temporary medicine," that is, as the means by which we acquire knowledge of truth. That faith is a gift from God. His Spirit works in our hearts and so renews and guides our will so that we can freely believe since no one can believe against his own will. That very faith is also present in the human mind, but thoughts redeemed by the Holy Spirit and submission to God in humility and repentance, stand in direct contradiction to the pride and arrogance of unredeemed reason.

Faith itself already presupposes knowledge of its object, since without such knowledge there would be no faith possible.

But since this knowledge precedes faith, it can only be considered to have a preliminary character and cannot be considered to be knowledge in the true sense. This can only be attributed to true knowledge which proceeds from faith. Faith is the means of acquiring knowledge. This is also true for natural science, which just as all human society, ought to build upon and proceed from faith. Yet still, this can be said to be particularly true for any branch of knowledge which has the knowledge of God as its object. For this reason, its foundational principle can be found in the words of the prophet: "without faith, there is no understanding." We believe the truth of God, even if it remains unattainable in our natural state, for by faith we are enabled to understand it. Faith and science, therefore, stand in the same relation to each other as conception and birth, tree and fruits, work and wages: knowledge is the fruit and wages of faith.

In proceeding from this principle, Augustine encouraged himself and others to employ reason to apply the truth already acquired through faith. God does not despise reason, as it is one of His gifts after all. The pagan science, even with all its errors, still managed to discover shadows of truth by utilizing the revelation of God provided through reason and nature. Christians are therefore to appreciate and appropriate that which is true in even pagan science. Accordingly, Augustine employed all his rational faculties in an attempt to prove the reality of ideas, the existence of God, the spiritual nature of the soul, and even the doctrine of the Trinity. Yet he still maintained that everything we believe cannot be regarded as demonstrably true, as many things even in the sciences are to be taken on faith alone, such as the very facts of history, for which we have most often to place our trust in the witnesses of men. He regarded true scientific knowledge as only pertaining to so-called eternal truths as these manifested through logic and mathematics. But apart from that, we never have anything which is not taken by faith, certainly not in theology. That which I know, I believe; but not all that I believe do I know. Oftentimes we can only argue that it is not foolish to believe in divine revelation, but foolish indeed to not believe it. Here on earth, we never ascend beyond faith, which will only be rewarded with knowledge through sight in heaven.

The Shortcomings Of The Traditional View

Upon these foundations the Christian philosophy of science was built, which stood for ages, which is in itself commendable. But even this human labor had its shortcomings, which in the long run became increasingly evident. Science, as it was practiced during the Middle Ages and thereafter also by Protestants up until the eighteenth century, suffered from one-sidedness and shortcomings that could not but contribute to its own decline. Firstly, faith and reason, even if at first harmoniously reconciled, were quickly and forcefully separated again—as if each of them brought their own set of truths to the table. It was argued that supernatural truths are to be accepted on authority, next to which there exist natural truths to be acquired through reason. Regarding the former, faith alone was needed; regarding only the latter, knowledge was possible. This led to some believing that their respective truths could be upheld in isolation from each other as if there was not a single unified truth so that that which is false in philosophy could still be true in theology and vice versa. But even if men thankfully mostly shied away from this consequence, this juxtaposition did effectuate a rivalry which in the end resulted in either suppressing reason in the name of revelation or suppressing revelation in the name of reason.

Its second shortcoming pertains to the fact that during this time science was often absolved in theology, and theology in dogmatics. During the first few centuries after Christ, it was philosophy which aided the development of theology. The expression that philosophy is the handmaid of theology, is not in itself doing a disservice to philosophy, since it is through philosophy that divine truth is applied to the field of science. But gradually this came to be understood in the sense that science ought to be deprived of its freedom of investigation and be reduced to nothing more than a servant of theology. And as such, in abusing its power, theology illegitimately expanded its terrain. Theology did not limit itself to the revealed knowledge of God, but expanded also to the scientific fields of psychology, cosmology, and metaphysics; it sought to provide answers to each and every possible question and to deliver a comprehensive worldview.

Hereunto we can also add a third shortcoming, namely the neglect of empirical evidence. The theory itself was solid: neither Protestants nor Roman Catholics ever claimed anything other than that cognitive knowledge begins with the observations of the senses. When Bacon appealed to experience as the source of science, he did not in fact proclaim anything new.[1] But as is so often the case, here too, theory did not fully correspond to practice. The naive assumption was that the ancients had already sufficiently exhausted all empirical evidence, and therefore the scholastics tried to collect all of their data for the various sciences from these sources alone, instead of utilizing fresh waters of knowledge. Philosophy was based in Aristotle, medicine in Hippocrates, mathematics in Euclides, Latin grammar in Donatus, rhetoric in Quintilian, music in Boethius, and theology in Lombard. Science

---

[1] The method applied by Bacon for scientific investigation had already in various degrees been applied by his peers such as Tycho Brahe, Kepler, Galileo, and others. Joseph de Maistre, therefore, says that Bacon, while proclaiming those great laws of science, wrongly believed that he had invented them.

became pure book knowledge and people forgot to observe with their own eyes. But we are not to overemphasize this shortcoming on the part of the scholastics either. Everything has its destined time and place. Natural science as we have come to know it had been, in earlier times, for various practical and technical reasons, impossible. Nonetheless, the neglect of experience was the kind of shortcoming that could not be without devastating consequences.

The reaction had already started during the period of transition between the Middle Ages and the modern era. This new era was not simply inaugurated by the Reformation, but the fertile ground for it was prepared by the rise of a free citizenry, the Renaissance, the awakening of science, the discovery of America, the development of trade, and that of navigation at sea. All these phenomena and events had a particular character, but they were all manifestations of the liberation from scholasticism and hierarchy. They all manifested the desire for liberty and a recognition of that which is natural because that which pertains to the natural was indeed suppressed during the Middle Ages, and not sanctified as it should have been. Yet it was eventually liberated from its bonds and enabled to take its rightful place.

Among all these important events, however, the Reformation distinguishes itself in terms of its distinctly religious and ethical objectives. It did not aim for the emancipation of man, yet it fought against Rome for the liberty of Christians. Nonetheless the strength of the Renaissance which arose independently of, yet also alongside it, did not allow itself to be prescribed by the principles of the Reformation. And so it happened, that the religious reformation was quickly stopped in its tracks and, to its own shame, had to be limited to the Church and to theology, while science increasingly strove towards the ideal of independence. Emancipation became its driving force—firstly emancipation from the Church and its confessions, but secondly also from Christianity and Scripture itself. For the time being its beneficence is also cautiously sought in this very separation. The idea was that theology and science could continue to co-exist peacefully as long as one did not interfere with the other. Faith, therefore, had to occupy itself with matters of theology and the Church, and science would refrain from attacking established doctrines. In the period following the Reformation, science at first by no means sought to establish itself upon the foundation of unbelief. It left theology to itself and based itself on its own metaphysical and rationalist dogmas. The ecclesiastical division which had manifested itself in the aftermath of the Reformation helped effectuate this as it drove many to seek a general and universal truth amid all the confusion. In religion, morality, and legal theory, the sum of rational truth was thereafter elevated to the chief principle and ultimate guideline. The theological phase of science was then, as per Comte, replaced by the metaphysical phase. While all realities had previously been interpreted as the acts of a personal God, men had come to believe in what Ludwig Stein would call "conditional thought," which causally identified all realities as the outworking of abstract essentials and natural laws. Descartes presupposed the existence of immutable and congenital ideas. Spinoza treated the entire cosmos as a geometric phenomenon, in which one aspect, as if by necessity, flows from the other. Leibniz conceived of the universe as the harmonious cooperation of metaphysical forces. Even the French Revolution had a distinctly dogmatic character and was based on the idea of abstractions as its standard and guide.

But this rationalistic dogmatism suffered a fatal blow at the hand of the Königsberg philosopher, Immanuel Kant. In order to make room for faith, he elevated knowledge to the level of metaphysics. Just like Bacon, he proposed a separation between faith and knowledge, not only for the sake of establishing peace but principally derived it from the implications of the human ability to acquire knowledge. He limited knowledge in accordance with this ability to that which is observable by virtue of the senses, but behind this, there was also an unknown land—a *terra incognita*—which provides faith with a refuge or asylum. This principle and radical separation on the part of Kant was based on an unproven apriorism, namely that our ability for knowledge *a priori* brings synthetical judgments along with it, and thus implies general and necessary knowledge of the phenomenal world. While neglecting the criticism and dualism on the part of Kant, the speculative philosophy of Fichte, Schelling, and Hegel appropriated this apriorism and built upon it. If I myself could be the creator of the phenomenological world, then there could be no objection to elevating and applying that principle to all of reality. The theoretical-recognitive idealism of Kant was developed by Fichte to an ethical idealism and pantheism, by Schelling to an aesthetical idealism and pantheism, and by Hegel to a logical idealism or pantheism.

The high regard this idealism gives to science and the university is seen not only in Kant's *Streit der Fakultäten*, in which he argues that the faculty of philosophy alone can claim to acquire genuine truth, but is even clearer from Fichte's *Plan einer zu Berlin zu errichtenden höheren Lehranstalt*, published in 1807. Therein he articulated the idea that the university not only forms an unmissable part of the national education but also has the duty to educate from science to science. In order to achieve this goal, it has to completely isolate itself from the everyday concerns of the general population and not be bothered by the earthly human struggle for survival. It has to be completely dedicated to the sacred cause of science, and it is ultimately called to transmit scientific knowledge from one generation to the next and train up men to take up the task of practicing science—thus the universities must not be centers of education but rather seminaries for future professors. Fichte desired to elevate the university to a center of all knowledge, and a factory for the idea of divinizing humanity. For him, the university was "the most sacred of all things humanity possesses, the visible manifestation of the Unity of the World, the manifestation of God Himself."

We are fortunate that this conception of science and the university is not applied in practice. The University of Berlin, for which Fichte had designed this plan, was instituted in a wholly different manner. The designer of her statutes, Wilhelm von Humboldt, did not construct this institution along philosophical categories, but, in consideration of reality, structured the university in such a way in order to enable it to produce good servants of both Church and state. Not only that, but the apriorist constructions of German Idealism also proved to be a major disappointment when it came to solving the practical challenges of life. At the same time, a historical movement was born that strove to explain natural phenomena with renewed vigor and, in its desire to be eminently practical, silenced all metaphysics, theology, and philosophy by advocating for the sole supremacy of the inductive method. In Germany, since there existed an aversion to materialism, there was also a return to the criticism of Kant. In France, the philosophy of Victor Cousin made way for that of Auguste Comte. In England, John Stuart Mill advocated for a rigorous empiricism and gradually the field of science was conceived of as the only one able to acquire absolute truth, and which boasted about being free from all presuppositions.

Positivism

According to the positivist narrative, science had previously been trapped in the theological and metaphysical phases but is currently progressing toward the positivist age. It conceives of the growth of knowledge in the same way it conceives of the growth of a human being, with an infant being stuck in the theological phase, progressing towards the metaphysical phase in his youth, but maturing to become a physicist. Currently, we have supposedly progressed so far that the positivists foresee the end of all that they consider childish, namely the fruitlessness and vanity that positivists associate with theology and metaphysical speculation. They have concluded that empirical investigation and the inductive method are the fundamentals of science, and that man has no business investigating whatever is either invisible or eternal or inquiring with regard to the ultimate cause of all things. Not only God and the divine nature, but also the essence, causes, and purpose of things, inasmuch as they have a metaphysical nature, lie beyond the realm of human knowledge.

Man is to limit himself to the study of phenomena observable through the senses and must make it his chief end to come to know these phenomena and their internal relationships, thereby discovering the laws which govern them each individually and together as a unified whole. In previous times, science was considered to be an investigation into the essence and cause of all things, a *rerum cognoscere causas*, but now it is conceived of as a desire for knowledge regarding the relationships between things, a *rerum cognoscere nexum*. And thus, while scholars in the past proposed an ascension from the visible to the invisible, from the temporary to the eternal, and from the relative to the absolute, in order to understand the *sub specie aeternitas*, contemporary science now only recognizes that which is relative, without recognition of an absolute principle.

This perspective undoubtedly results in scientific decline, since it remains willingly ignorant of everything which underlies or causes the phenomena it seeks to explain. It can say nothing about it, neither positive nor negative, and is therefore doomed to abstentionism and agnosticism regarding all that cannot be observed through the senses. All of this, if it exists at all, must be conceded to the category of subjective opinions. Whosoever desires to occupy this unknown territory can do so by means of his postulates, his subjective judgments, the creations of his imagination, the ideals of his sentiments, or with the fantasies of his religion. In this unknown territory, there is even a place for ghosts, deceased spirits, and demonic powers. Positivism allows for religiosity, the cult of humanity, for the veneration of the deceased, for an altar to the unknown god, and even for the worship of Satan. All of this, after all, in no way pertains to science and is a purely private matter in which each can do as he pleases.

But what science loses in terms of terrain or territory, it gains, according to the positivists, in terms of internal certainty. Because as long as it limits itself to that which is observable through the senses and the internal relationships of phenomena, it can reach a point where the present can be explained in light of the past and the future predicted in light of both. And that is the ideal of this modern science. Just like through astronomy the future phenomena of space can be predicted, so science ought to be able to predict the future in light of observable facts. While religion thus remains a private matter, in public we are only to deal with that which is positively demonstrable, and only that which science claims to be true is to be taken into consideration. In the past, the Church and state authoritatively announced their teachings, but from now on science, represented by an Areopagus of experts, must determine that which is to guide public life. They are to be what Ludwig Stein calls the "Rulers of the Future" who are to guide the "advancement of humanity." In previous times, religion held all the power, but as Malvert puts it: "Now it is science, as the ultimate expression of truth, which is called to rule the world. Science is to be the god of the world, the redeemer of nations, and the liberator of mankind."

This is currently the prevalent notion in the scientific community, even if very few are conscious of the doctrine of science to which they adhere. They maintain that this conception of science is settled and immune to criticism and are wholly surprised whenever anyone dares to question this doctrine or seriously resists it. They are held captive by their notion of an unprejudiced scientific doctrine and declare this to be absolute, whereas everything else is considered to be relative. This is also the opinion even of Mr. Levy, who is himself no friend of positivism, namely that no one apparently conceives of science in any way apart from its complete distinction from faith. Nonetheless, despite his emphasis of the dichotomy, he still argues for a nuanced definition of science, albeit not for a nuanced conceptualization thereof, as if the two stood in no relation to each other.

In the same spirit, a writer by the name of Q.N. argues in a recent newspaper article that:

> Only that which is the result of an unprejudiced search for truth is to be considered scientific. While it is true that all human endeavors make use of certain presuppositions which, in

accordance with their spirit, pave the way for those endeavors. Science itself can also in no way be free from presuppositions and we could not demand it to be so. But there is a difference between presuppositions and prejudices, and the need for science to remain free from prejudices can never be emphasized enough. Those who desire to practice it must remain fully unconcerned about where it will lead. The true scientist proceeds without any idea of where he will end ... those with a preconceived idea of where their journey will end do no service to true science but betray it.

Professor Groenewegen from the University of Leiden agrees with this sentiment, arguing that science is methodically structured, thereby resulting in satisfactory and objective knowledge. But there is no science that does not proceed from presuppositions. These presuppositions, either as principles or as hypotheses, enable and structure scientific research. Furthermore, the human mind never operates as a lifeless machine and therefore cannot liberate itself from influences or desires. Even the most sober thinker would never be able to liberate himself from the preconceived convictions intimately connected to his soul. But the scientific man only utilizes these presuppositions as long as they serve his scientific purposes and lets go of them as soon as they are revealed to be untenable. Groenewegen argues that neutrality in the sense of being free from any pre-investigative commitments is either impossible or, inasmuch as it is possible, sinful. But he maintains that neutrality in the sense of objectivity with regard to the traditional convictions in comparison with one's own is both scientific and a religious duty.

Assessment Of Positivism

When we assess the positivist conception of science, we encounter several problems. It is after all evident that the description provided by Professor Groenewegen—i.e., that science is nothing but the result of methodically acquired, proven, and trustworthy knowledge— is of no use, since no one would not agree with such a definition. The question, however, is what the normative method for the acquisition of knowledge is and when knowledge can be called proven and trustworthy. Furthermore, the distinction which the writer Q.N. makes, namely between lawful presuppositions and unlawful prejudices, is not in itself capable of casting light upon the matter at hand. Because again, no one would not accept such a distinction. Both Protestant and Roman Catholic scholars, who recognize the confession of their Church as authoritative based on divine authority, maintain that it is precisely this truth which keeps us from descending into heresy and also forms the best framework for enabling unprejudiced research. And, after all, this can be no other way; truth liberates. If we were for one moment to assume that the righteous are justified in regarding Holy Scripture as the Word of God, then it follows that scientific investigation can in no way be inhibited thereby, but that it is, in fact, this very belief which guides it on the path of truth, whereas the rejection of God's Word, in fact, amounts to a prejudice most damaging to scientific inquiry. This truth is amplified by the fact that it is undeniable that the men of science perpetually err, constantly disagree with each other, and periodically revise the results of their investigations. A truth that therefore guides science in preserving it from error cannot in the name of fighting prejudice or promoting unbiased research be put aside but must rather be graciously accepted.

But the modernists deny the authority of Scripture and resist the idea of a special divine revelation. But this cannot prove decisive in terms of the question at hand. If one were to reduce a science based upon the acceptance of divine revelation to mere prejudice, the matter would be settled of course, but such a view would be in itself guilty of *petitio principii—* that is, of *a priori* assuming a premise to be true without it being proven to be so. It is, after all, the very existence of a special divine revelation that is in dispute. If God has, through special inspiration, revealed knowledge of Himself, then it goes without saying that science has to take this into account and that failing to do so would amount to disobedience and heresy. On the other hand, of course, if no such revelation exists, then adherence to such a concept would amount to an unlawful prejudice. Nonetheless, the acceptance or rejection thereof is ultimately not a scientific but a religious matter, not of the mind but of the heart. And therefore, science cannot simply unilaterally place itself on one side of this debate and condemn the alternative as unscientific. While there have in the past certainly been Christian scientists who have made themselves guilty of unjust prejudices, the same can be said, in equal degree, of irreligious scientists. So often a hatred of God and of religion, of Christ and of Scripture, of the Church and her confession is confused for clarity of mind and objective thought. Even liberal theologians must admit this, as they cannot deny the existence of nor approve of the contempt for religion which so often characterizes the worldview of the men of science. After all, they still believe in the objective truth of religion and the existence and knowability of God. But such a faith is for the positivist as well as the materialist as qualitatively and scientifically foolish as is believing in the existence of a special revelation. Why then is it that the liberals always seem to attack the faithful and claim to fight for science, while they are themselves rejected just as much as orthodox Christians are? In the battle against modern science, it is not only the nature of faith in a special revelation that is in dispute, but the very existence of objective truth itself, and consequently also religion's right to continued existence.

It is evident that the very contrast between science and dogma is untenable even to modernist theologians. Because if one is truly a theologian, he still holds to the idea of religious truth and the existence of God, which makes him in the eyes of positivists a dogmatist. Whether someone stands with science or with dogmatism is completely dependent upon the perspective of the one categorizing him. Objectively drawing a definite line between science and dogma is both practically and theoretically impossible. Of this Professor Groenewegen himself is a perfect example. He acknowledges that even the most sober researcher cannot separate himself from pre-investigative commitments. Yet he immediately adds that reevaluating the literary, scientific, and philosophical ideas historically associated with Christianity amounts to no indifference to truth, while it indeed amounts to indifference to truth whenever only that which is in accordance with the faith is held to be genuine knowledge while all else is declared anathema. However, in reality, this last proposition of his is indeed anathema, pronounced by liberals against those who, in their opinion, cling to dogma at the cost of science—an accusation that amounts to nothing less than indifference towards truth. As a matter of fact, Professor Groenewegen's entire argument amounts to this: that the man of science ought not to give up the modern, but rather the orthodox religious conceptions. And this argument is quite common. No one can deny that any scientific researcher brings along with him a host of religious, moral, and philosophical presuppositions by which he is more or less guided. But every party claims that their presuppositions are right and useful and those of opposing parties false. The Roman Catholics and the Protestants, the Lutherans and the Reformed, and the orthodox and the liberals all proclaim themselves to be objective and their opponents to be prejudiced. Their respective historiographies bear clear evidence thereof. It is, therefore, presumptuous for one party to promote itself as the sole representative of true science while reducing all other positions to dogmatism since the issue causing division is precisely the debate regarding what constitutes illegitimate prejudice and what constitutes legitimate presuppositions.

The dividing line between the two cannot be either theoretically or practically drawn. No single party dares to claim that other parties have contributed absolutely nothing in the field of science. No single school will dare go as far as to say that truth is found in them alone while others have exclusively conjured up falsehoods. But still, the tone taken by the modernists against orthodox believers for decades now has been exceptionally prideful and audacious.

Thankfully, this is also gradually changing. Many now acknowledge that in the past the representatives of their position have been overly one-sided and that professors representing differing positions ought to be appointed at universities since among the faithful there are also a number of exceptional scientists. No liberal scholar who does not vehemently cling to his own dogma would deny the exceptional contributions of both Protestant and Roman Catholic researchers in terms of philosophical, scientific, historical, or literary scholarship. On the other hand, Christians have never been so narrow-minded as to reject any and all scientific contributions of unbelievers as wholly false. Since the first centuries, we have appreciated classical philosophy and literature. We have selected and weighed it, consequently embraced that which is good, and continued to apply it fruitfully. And who among us would even consider disregarding the contemporary efforts and sacrifices made by non-believing researchers? All without distinction now enjoy the most pleasant benefits of the most genius inventions and most surprising discoveries of our time. Christians have no reason to look down upon these scientific discoveries because we believe that God, the same God we confess to be our Father in Christ, allows the sun to shine over the righteous and the unrighteous. All good and perfect gifts come to us from the Father of lights, with whom there is no variation nor shadow of turning. If we were to remain unthankful for these gifts, however, we would in fact do an injustice to humanity and stand guilty before God.

Religion and science, faith and knowledge, purity of heart and clarity of the mind, undoubtedly stand in relation to each other just like sins and lies, injustice and heresy, an immoral lifestyle and a false doctrine. That relationship is often even closer than we are prone to admit. Francois Coppée even later in life admitted that it was by virtue of his Christian upbringing that he was preserved from falling into the heresies of youth. And many, he says, would, if they were to be honest, admit that it is the strict moral laws associated with religion that originally alienated them from religion, those same laws they, once they matured, desired to deconstruct in order to justify disobedience to them by means of a scientific method. However, as close as the relationship between faith and science may be, they are not the same. He who believes in Christ is not necessarily a scientist, and he who rejects Christ is not necessarily a liar or mentally incompetent. Believers can in terms of their natural ability often rank far lower than unbelievers. Among some Christians, there can even be found a narrow-minded dogmatism, while some non-Christians can be very open-minded.

But all of this in no way confirms the positivist notion of science. The first thing the advocates of positivism need to learn is that their conception of science is but one among many. Every school of course advocates their own position as the sole truth, and the reason for this is quite obvious, since if they hadn't done so they would be admitting that they do not truly believe that which they advocate. But we can still admit that our view is not the only one which exists in the world and that other views enjoy equal rights in practice. If we were to refuse to admit this, we would become exclusive and intolerant, and not far removed from the point of suppressing all those who disagree with us through violence. But such a course of action would be at odds with both science and truth because truth can never rule through violence and compulsion, through civil authority or ecclesiastical force, but only by means of an ethical way: through the conviction of its internal power and the strength of its arguments. Mr. Levy accuses Dr. Kuyper that he is a representative of ecclesiastical absolutism in the same way that Hobbes was of secular absolutism. But such an accusation only proves that Mr. Levy is so caught up in his own dogma that he is unable to comprehend the position of his opponents. The battle for free Christian education, of which Kuyper is the leading representative, after all, centers around the very idea that one scientific school should not exercise a monopoly in the field, and that the different schools should be able to develop freely within a society in which the state does not privilege one over the other so as to make concurrence impossible.

It is of course possible that the state itself has a set confession that it maintains in and through all public institutions. But liberalism itself has vehemently resisted this, neutralized the public domain, and declared all Churches, confessions, and religions equal. If there is a large portion of the population that, on the basis of this declaration, requests equal rights for the Church, the Christian school, and the Christian university, liberals are supposed to support it if they were to remain true to their own principles, but in practice, they almost always oppose it. That is the contradiction in which it so often places itself, and why it so often comes across as liberal in word, but not in deed. Their principle seems to fear its own application. This was shown to be the case in the battle for elementary education, and now again in discussions surrounding secondary education. It is precisely this so-called "presuppositionless" science it advocates that suppresses the rights of all other convictions and demands sole sovereignty, claiming all state sanction and funding for itself. This scientific school needs to come to the realization that the positivist view of science is but one among many. It may of course not surrender its claim to absolute truth, but it should at least cease using unethical means of promoting its position. It should learn to tolerate those who disagree with its position and instead advocate a radically different conception of science. This is because the difference effectuated by contrasting worldviews as well as moral and religious convictions not only becomes applicable when it comes to scientific methods and findings but is already most relevant when defining the very concept of science itself. The concept of what science is can, after all, not be derived from experience or observation. It is not the result of empirical investigation, but of a philosophical idea intrinsically tied to one's worldview.

A Continued Assessment Of Positivism

The concept of a "presuppositionless science" is apparently the fruit of positivist philosophy. This worldview is just as much a philosophical system as that of Plato or Aristotle, Schelling, or Hegel. And positivism is certainly not only an abstraction but rather the philosophical worldview of a particular thinker and those who strive to follow him. This particular philosophy arose around the middle of the nineteenth century, and would now, only half a century later, already have lost all credibility had it not recently been revived under a different name and in a different form by Richard Avenarius, who has managed to convince quite a few of the strength of this position. The empiricists also maintain that their position, which rests exclusively on experience to the exclusion of all transcendence, is alone truthful. But even this school has been condemned by none other than psychologist Wilhelm Wundt with regard to the fact that it does not accept experience without bias, but rather, like the scholastics, interprets this experience in light of a given metaphysical conception. Various scholars have also accused this school of relativism and subjectivism with regard to logic, ethics, and religion because of its reduction of all things to mere psychological phenomena—a position that ultimately leads to the destruction of all knowledge and complete skepticism.

It is by no means difficult to see how skepticism is essentially a distinct philosophy that, just like all others, proceeds from certain metaphysical presuppositions. In fact, it is not even possible to have a theory of knowledge without metaphysics and philosophy, and anyone who advocates any position in this regard either consciously or subconsciously adheres to such a philosophy and theory of metaphysics. For this reason, Allard Pierson, in his work entitled *Worldview* rightly speaks of foundational philosophical principles when addressing the origin, nature, and limits of human knowledge. And the first philosophical principle he identifies is that knowledge has no true origin apart from our experience and observation through the senses. This is indeed a philosophical presupposition, and not a self-evident one, but rather one based on an entire worldview, which is only accepted by relatively few people as the standard of truth. The history of mankind bears witness to the fact that, in terms of scientific investigation, other philosophical principles dominated. And it would be very naive to believe that this principle forms the sure foundation for undoubted knowledge about reality.

We have now shown that all scientific investigation presupposes without evidence the reliability of the senses as well as the objectivity of that which they observe. This is an unprovable axiom. Whosoever doubts this, cannot be convinced by any argument. Skepticism is a matter of the heart but not of the mind. The reality of the world must be accepted upon a faith in the reliability of the senses. Accepting the reality of creation is an act of trust, and the foundation of all trust is the truthfulness of God. After all, knowledge of the world outside of us can only be acquired by sensual experience, and we have no way of comparing this experience to the reality outside of ourselves since we are unable to escape ourselves. We must simply believe that our observations and experience correspond to true knowledge of reality.

Observation through the senses is by no means as simple as many claim it to be. A purely objective observer does not exist, as Pierson also rightly points out. Firstly, there is no observer who is also a person and whose observations are not dependent upon and informed by his condition and position. It is, after all, not the eye or the ear which observes, but the person who utilizes these senses. Observation itself is a psychological action, and not a passive but an active one in which the interpretation of the subject is decisive. Constituting facts is a subjective action. This subjectivity is even more prominent in the process of relating observations to one another. In actual fact, any observation in itself already constitutes an interpretation and correlation of various findings. Many of our words are names of objects which cannot be observed. We do not observe anything which can solely be considered a dog or a chair, for example, but we combine various observations and thereby form a concept of a dog or a chair, thereby simultaneously classifying various objects in certain categories by means of our observations through which we recognize similarities.

In other words, without cognitive interpretation, there can be no observations in the scientific sense. This activity, when it comes to scientific research, is in fact threefold. First, the mind directs the senses in a particular direction, selects a set group of phenomena, and isolates it from the rest of the universe, thereafter, abstracting and combining each observed phenomenon with others. Secondly, when it comes to scientific interpretation, a whole host of presuppositions and perspectives come into play. Already Aristotle saw that there should not only be a mediated but an immediate form of knowledge. Even in rejecting Plato's idealism and instead deriving all knowledge from experience, he realized that all proof ultimately should rest upon an unprovable, foundational truth. The proofs themselves would have to be traced back to those propositions which are immediately true. All science, therefore, proceeds from certain axiomata. And thirdly, the outworking of thought also consists in identifying the relationship, idea, and law behind phenomena, thereby discovering real scientific facts. It, therefore, presupposes the often unspoken belief that in the phenomena a certain unity, order, and reason exist, to which humanity must submit. In full confidence, it can therefore apply not only the laws of logic, but also various metaphysical concepts such as element, characteristic, cause, effect, law, condition, time, space, truth, and falsehood to observed phenomena. For scientific research this is inescapable, and therefore proves its need for philosophy and metaphysics.

Positivism, therefore, proves itself to be untenable even when it comes to observations made through the senses. But it is even more thoroughly refuted by looking towards internal human experience. Comte, Avenarius, and many of the new psychologists deny the independence and unique nature thereof, as well as its role as a source of knowledge apart from sensual experience. It cannot be denied, of course, that the distinction between external and internal experience takes time to be fully recognized by our consciousness, and also that the observations of realities outside of ourselves can only be internally processed. But gradually it does become evident that the distinction between these two kinds of phenomena is a necessary one. There is, after all, a great difference between conceptions of things that reflect themselves through observations in our consciousness on the one hand, and these same conceptions as the result of our own psychological activity. And along with this comes all the imagination, affections, and desires which, though not isolated from external influences, are not the product of anything outside of us, but of our own internal consciousness.

With these facts of our own consciousness in mind, we can easily identify the distinction between the physical and the psychological, between object and subject, and between matter and spirit. Of course, hereby it is not denied that these always stand in a close relationship to each other and that consciousness itself is effectuated by physical organs and bodily functions. But even if that relationship were to be shown to be even more proximate by physiological psychology, the distinction between the two would never be invalidated. After all, we have knowledge of both visible and invisible realities, and we are all conscious of truths, propositions, influences, and dispositions which cannot be observed by means of the senses, but the existence of which is undeniable. There are facts with regard to the human soul which we regard to be equally sure, and perhaps even more sure than empirical phenomena, and there are forces at work in our consciousness that are much stronger than any physical force, such as dispositions, heart's desires, convictions, and decisions of the will. These are just as real as any physical reality, even if they cannot be seen by our eyes or touched with our hands. And because this is true, it cannot be maintained that only that which we can observe by means of our senses truly exists or can constitute the sole object of scientific investigation.

In fact, many have tried to modify the positivist position in terms of acknowledging not only physical but also psychological realities, thereby acknowledging not only external but also internal experience as a source of knowledge. But they still maintain that even on the level of the spiritual only the empirical method can be maintained, thereby still denying the existence of *a priori* presuppositions and any kind of commitments of faith. And of course, here again, we can raise the same objection against empiricism and its method which I had briefly mentioned earlier. Because for such a method, one should presuppose the reliability of our senses and certain laws of logic, and the acceptance of the reality of the physical world, which is itself an unproven axiom. The very hypothesis, that there exists order and rules, logic and laws in the psychological world is a commitment of faith standing upon the conviction of the truthfulness of God alone.

A further objection is that the empirical-deductive method cannot be objectively or fruitfully applied to the psychological realm—even less than it can in the study of natural phenomena. The soul and nature of man are, after all, so incredibly complex and diverse that they can never be reduced to an object of scientific investigation. In order to speak of any kind of scientific inquiry into psychological phenomena, all of these phenomena would have to be isolated from each other and independently studied. The research would have to begin by isolating the phenomenon it wishes to study from the relationships in which it manifests as a reality. It would have to start by abstracting it, but such an abstraction is in and of itself an activity of reason, which guides and structures the very observation of that particular phenomenon. And apart from that, the spiritual life of man is furthermore so rich and complex that there would never be an end to the innumerable observations made, as long as the light of reason does not shed light upon it and bring chaos to order. The empirical method is therefore valuable and good, but it must be recognized that this is cognitively guided and structured from beginning to end.

The greatest objection against this application of positivism, however, arises when one asks the question of what the end of such an investigation of psychological phenomena is. If it is only aimed at acquiring knowledge of psychological processes and their origin, relationships, differences, and distinct development among different individuals, nations, or humanity as a whole, then everything in the field of humanities would be reduced to psychology. But that is quite contrary to the original intentions of the field of humanities itself. The goal had always been to ascend from subjective representation to objective truth. This also applies to all of our observations, by which external realities are reflected back upon us. The idea has never been to simply understand the psychological processes behind representations of the world, but to come to know the world itself by means of such representations. And with regard to those representations which do not point back to natural phenomena observable by the senses, the same principle applies. They too point back to a reality, albeit not an observable but a spiritual reality. Our consciousness is capable of findings, realizations, and representations that point back to truth, goodness, and aesthetics. Of course, such realizations can also be investigated in terms of their psychological nature, but through this, we would only be able to acquire knowledge of one empirical reality which exists in the subject alone. But as natural science and historiography pertain not to knowledge of human representations of natural and historical phenomena and processes, but to those processes and phenomena themselves, so I argue that, also, investigation into psychology should not be limited to mere representations of the psychological realities and processes, but knowledge of the spiritual world itself, of which human representation is always but an impure imprint thereof. All those who maintain this understanding of the field of humanities necessarily have to forsake empiricism and positivism for the realm of ideas—that is, the fields of ontology and metaphysics. There are of course many scholars who provide no account of their method. They often speak as if the empirical-deductive method is the only one there is, but then conveniently go on to apply the synthetic-deductive method when necessary. But this shows that scientific investigation itself is at odds with the empirical-positivist conception thereof. One cannot claim that scientific research proceeds from a completely objective standpoint, only taking into account that which can be demonstrated by observation either externally or internally, while at the same time bringing along a set of presuppositions that aren't themselves the fruits of empirical investigation but have a distinctly philosophical and metaphysical character. One cannot claim that scientific knowledge can only be deducted from unbiased observation as the sole source of truth, while simultaneously acknowledging the existence of certain logical, ethical, religious, or aesthetic norms. Either there is only an empirical and historical reality, and religion becomes nothing but a psychological phenomenon, and there is also no logic or any ethics, no truth and no virtue, no beauty and no justice—then true and false representations carry equal legitimacy and are both necessary and both ultimately the products of the development of our representations, just like good and evil deeds are then merely the necessary result of innate and acquired dispositions—or there are absolute norms and over and above empirical reality there exists a world of ideas, a realm of goodness, truth, and beauty—but then the positivist and empiricist notions of science cannot be upheld.

This has been partially acknowledged by the very proponents of this view themselves, inasmuch as they have limited the terrain of scientific investigation to one surrounded by a *terra incognita*. In their attempt to avoid descending into materialism, positivism has sought redemption in silence and ignorance. But this has not improved their case. Because even in the terrain to which it limits itself, it remains not only subject to the aforementioned criticisms, but a further internal inconsistency arises. The claim that all that is ontological and metaphysical is unknowable, has significant scientific implications. In order to acknowledge it as unknowable, one has to have some concept of what it is. Anyone who claims that God, truth, goodness, and beauty cannot be known, at the same time declares that he believes in their existence and that he has some knowledge of them—enough at least to be able to legitimately claim that he does not know them. Agnosticism is therefore, properly speaking, internally inconsistent, as it is either itself dependent upon a very distinct theistic conception, or it is forced to deny all absolutes, which would then reduce it to merely a less reprehensible name for atheism and materialism.

In conclusion, we must still draw our attention to two very different objects that positivism consistently confuses with one another. When it claims that "everything is relative, which alone is absolute," then this of course implies that literally all of our knowledge of both visible and non-visible things is insufficient. All knowledge is partial and preliminary. But Comte himself has not acknowledged this implication. There is a great distinction between the characteristics of our knowledge of any given object and the characteristics of that object itself. Nothing concerning the latter can be deduced from the former. There is no contradiction in the idea on the one hand that the absolute exists, and on the other hand that our knowledge of that absolute is not absolute. That which is relative does not as objects of knowledge become absolute by virtue of us acquiring absolute knowledge thereof, just like that which is absolute does not become relative by virtue of our relative, preliminary, and limited knowledge thereof. There is no problem with acknowledging the relativity of our knowledge as long as we do not use this to deny the existence of the absolute. That which truly know, is very little, as Kant and Comte have convincingly shown. They have, however, just like the scholastics, failed by virtue of their sharp distinction between what can be precisely and objectively known and that which can be believed on subjective grounds. The distinction between the two cannot be proven. The world cannot thus be divided into two halves, nor a man into two distinct persons. As Hermann Ulrici in his *Gott und die Natur* has pointed out:

> If we were to remove from science all that which is in truth axioms accepted on faith, its entire contents would be reduced to a few partial sentences, the content of which is so insignificant that it is hardly worth studying.

One cannot pinpoint the moment where faith ends and knowledge begins. The inductive method is always guided by the deductive method. Underlying all scientific investigations are metaphysical presuppositions. This is because non-visible realities are manifested and revealed in visible realities, and the latter, properly understood, always leads to the former. Even of God, who is the origin of all things, we have some knowledge, and even the little that we know from His works are revealed by further investigation to be an inscrutable mystery.

2

The Concept Of Science

In order to come to a clear understanding of the essence and purpose of science, we cannot do any better than proceeding from empirical knowledge. After all, being precedes reason. Mankind had lived for centuries before investigating the biological dynamics of life. We had been capable of thought prior to laying down the foundations of reason and logic. We spoke and developed language before anyone bothered studying the laws of grammar. We participated in a rich religious, moral, legal, and political life before the development of any theory regarding the nature of this life. We developed agriculture, industry, and trade before any scientific investigation into these phenomena was even started. Everywhere, life precedes philosophy. Scientific knowledge may be considered the greatest fruit of human activity, but it is most certainly not the root from which life sprung. The existence of human culture itself of course also necessitates the existence of the knowledge of religion, morality, law, aesthetics, politics, society, industry, agriculture, etc., in the human consciousness, but this had all been based on thoughts, conceptions, and realizations. But such empirical knowledge is the fruit of the kind of observation and practical experience which is intrinsically tied to human wisdom and therefore acquirable by all.

This empirical knowledge is of the highest value as the condition and foundation of all human life. Therefore, it would be most inappropriate to reject it. Those who are immediately skeptical thereof and expect certainty from scientific investigation alone undermine the very foundation upon which science rests. Within the realm of empirical knowledge, we find not only that which can be seen but also that which is invisible and spiritual. We do not only know from experience that the sun rises in the east and sets in the west, or that the years and seasons follow each other in a consistent fashion, but we also know the distinction between truth and falsehood, between good and evil, between justice and injustice; we know that stealing is a sin that requires punishment and that it is not permissible to do anything that contradicts our conscience. The concept of knowledge is also without hesitation applied to religious and moral convictions: the Christian knows that his Redeemer lives, that death is but a transition to eternal life, and that we will inherit salvation.

But still, we know from experience that the foundations of knowledge differ from case to case and that there are differing degrees of certainty and knowledge. Therefore, it is common to acknowledge the distinction between opinion, knowledge, and belief. An opinion is a belief held upon grounds which the subject holding that opinion is unconvinced of the reliability thereof; it is a kind of knowledge of which the subject himself is uncertain. In contradistinction, knowledge is something that is objectively evident and subjectively certain and is based upon foundations that are believed to be embraced by all, such as observation and evidence, and which brings about a certainty that excludes all doubt. Faith is to be distinguished from both. In general, faith is that by which a subject holds true something which in particular circumstances seems sufficiently evident so as to reasonably exclude doubt. This is a kind of knowledge that is not objectively evident to everyone but is subjectively sure. Not in subjective certainty but in terms of objective evidence, faith stands below knowledge. Everyone realizes this when they consider the meaning of statements such as "I believe it is so," "I believe it is going to rain," and "I believe that Mr. X is an honest man." The idea is always that I propose this belief, but I am not certain of it. In the same sense, believing can also be understood in the religious and moral sense: if two persons dispute with one another concerning the evidence for God's existence, the immortality of the soul, or the divinity of Christ, then faith or rejection thereof is nothing more than convictions held upon grounds considered subjectively sufficient.

For life itself, this faith has extensive meaning, since far and away most of our knowledge is acquired apart from our own observations, research, or argumentation, but through faith, by holding things to be true upon what we consider to be sufficient subjective grounds. In itself, this is not a problem. The contents of that which we believe through faith can be just as true as knowledge acquired by our own research and investigation. Everything depends upon the nature of the foundations upon which our faith rests. One of the most common and renowned foundations is the witness of another. We believe that which we could not have observed ourselves, but which we know from the reliable witness of others. Everything outside of my own line of sight—be that from the past, the present, or the future—can only become my knowledge by means of the witness of another who knows something about it and shares his knowledge. If his witness is shown to be reliable, the truth of his witness becomes my knowledge through faith. Our own observations and the witness of others—reason and authority—are two sources by which, in this life, we acquire knowledge: *Per visionem et fidem ad intellectum*.[2]

This empirical knowledge by which mankind has gradually, by experience, established the foundations of domestic and civil life, as well as religion and morality, does not prove to be sufficient in the long run. Once a certain level of civilization has been reached, once a class emerges that does not have to work for their daily bread, once the functions and utility of the senses have been exhausted, then the desire gradually arises to provide a systematic account of what has been experienced. Empirical knowledge oftentimes only touches the surface, and therefore

---

[2] On a religious level, we need to conceive of faith a little differently. Anyone, in comparing these two statements: 1) "All things considered, I believe that God exists, that He is omnipotent, and that He created the world," and 2) "I believe in God the Father Almighty, Maker of heaven and earth," knows that in the first instance, we are dealing with a historical faith, in which the existence of God and His creation is embraced as a scientific reality after evaluating the evidence for and against it. In the second case, we are dealing with a salvific faith expressing its confession. This faith cannot be considered true or false on the basis of cognitive reasoning but is dependent upon a full reliance upon God, and His revelation of Himself, and an embrace of His Word as His Word, and His promises. It is a personal confession that He is also my God and my Father. This faith does not rank lower than knowledge but is different from knowledge: it is a personal relationship with God, knowing Him as my God in Christ by means of His revelation.

mankind has committed itself to investigate reality methodically. An interest arises with regard to not only what is, but why it is so. Therefore, we trace the origins and development of phenomena even without regard for their practical and daily use, and for the sole purpose of understanding their place in reality and relation to other realities. Once mankind reaches the stage of not only being content with observation and acceptance but starting investigation and inquiry, science is truly born.

The concept of science is therefore always understood in a twofold manner, that is, as scientific inquiry and scientific results. A scientific subject is, after all, not only considered as such when its objectives have been reached and its truths have been exhausted. Thus understood, there would be no field of study that we would rightly be able to call scientific. Most fields are still stuck in the empirical phase—that is, there is acquired knowledge of most of the phenomena and facts but of their origin, meaning, laws, and purpose, there is still great ignorance. And this is by no means only true of theology and philosophy, as the same can be said of literature and history as well as of the natural and medical sciences. Medicine is still wholly stuck in the empirical stage, while physics and chemistry have developed to the point where they acknowledge the existence of a world of mystery. As soon as in the fields of science and history, religion and ethics, economics and sociology, a law is discovered, it is again challenged by the discovery of new phenomena. Therefore, by science, we do not understand anything more than scientific inquiry or investigation, whether that be viewed from the perspective of the subject doing the investigation or the object being investigated.

That which falls within the scope of scientific inquiry and which can rightly claim the name science, cannot be determined by us *a priori* but is gradually identified by the history of scholarship. Gradually, the scope of scientific investigation and the role of the university have been expanded. It was in ancient Greece when scholars started to inquire regarding the origin and foundation of things, that science started, and it was developed through further inquiry from there. During the medieval period, universities were not artificially erected by means of a preconceived plan, but gradually and organically developed and grew out of the development of scholarship. Nowadays even technical fields are elevated to the level of the university, as they are so rapidly evolving. The history of science is therefore one of gradual and organic development. This process itself will eventually become an object of scientific inquiry, as mankind seeks to discover the idea and rationale behind this development itself.

This development also shows us the vast difference between scientific and empirical knowledge. Empirical knowledge is limited to phenomena as they appear independently, but scientific knowledge pertains to the origin, meaning, cause, and purpose of phenomena as well as their relationship to the whole. Empirical knowledge is limited to what is experienced; science asks questions regarding why and how these phenomena came to be. The value of empirical knowledge is inseparable from its practical utility, while scientific knowledge strives towards knowledge of the truth. The distinction is similar to the distinction between the farmer who works the land and the agronomist who has made a study of the soil and its production, or the distinction between a man who knows many people and a psychologist, between a jury and a lawyer, or a Christian and a theologian.

But even with these distinctions, their interrelationships cannot be denied. Science, even in its highest development, needs to remain tied to life itself. It would not be wise to place science upon a purely theoretical pedestal, since those who practice it are mere humans who cannot live by oxygen alone. There would be many more great scientists if the practice of science had not been considered to be some kind of elevated calling or a completely independent existence. And by this, I do not mean that all science should be aimed merely at ensuring physical survival. After all, the acquisition of a professorship that ensures a stable income ensures that the practice of science can proceed unimpeded, since liberty from the need to worry about your daily bread is, as a rule, necessary for the development of good science. A good laborer completes his daily task to which he is obliged by virtue of the need to maintain himself, but he also develops a distinct love and passion for his work and his achievements. A work of art is often the result of an unstinted life, and scientists, just as much as artists, cannot be expected to practice for the love of their field alone.

But it is even more important to realize that any scientist is also still only a human being, not only in the physical sense of being, like all other humans, dependent on food and drink as well as clothing and shelter but also in the moral and religious sense. A chemist who knows the precise nutritional value of a dish is not fed by his knowledge, but by eating the dish itself. Likewise, the scientist can only remain religious and moral when he is fed with the same spiritual bread which alone can suffice for the spiritual hunger of the poorest and most uneducated laborer. In this regard, there is no distinction between the most learned scholar and the simplest citizen. They both share the same human nature. In both, the same depraved heart and will, the same wondering mind and sinful desires, can be found. Both also share the same religious needs, are bound by the same moral laws, and are destined for the same judgment. Those who realize this can understand that while science has an important role to play in human life, it is by no means all-encompassing. Alongside it, religion, morality, and art maintain their rightful place: science will never be able to replace these, not in the lives of the common people, and not in the lives of even the most dedicated scientists.

The sources from which scientists gain their knowledge are also the same sources used by all empirical studies. If the man of science remains only a human in the fullest sense of the word, then it becomes evident that true science can never be at odds with true religion, true morality, or with true art. Perhaps it can aid in clarifying these other fields, but it can never be considered to be their foundation or their replacement. Agriculture, trade, and industry are, in many regards, indebted to science, but their very existence is due to created elements in the world that exists independently of science. The same can be said of religion and morality, law and authority, beauty and art. They all have an independent existence, are subject to their own laws, and have their own purpose. The duty of science, however, is to acknowledge the full richness of life and to conceive of it in terms of its essence and truth.

This is not to say, of course, that science is simply supposed to take over and apply the findings of empirical research uncritically. After all, knowledge acquired through observation and experience is by no means infallible—in fact, it is just as fallible as the folk wisdom we find in common sayings. The empirical findings regarding agriculture, trade, religion, morality, law, and art must be constantly scrutinized by science so that they may be further clarified and improved. Any farmer who stubbornly maintains the old ways without recognizing the need for improvement is foolish. But the man of science likewise acts foolishly when he disregards practical experience and attempts to theorize without any regard for practice. A lawyer who fails to take into account the legal status and development of the nation would not be equipped for the legislature. The doctor who looks down on practical experiences forgets that his medical expertise relies on precisely that. As well, the theologian who disregards the religious convictions and dispositions of the faithful undermines the very foundation of his scholarship.

A prideful attitude on the part of science towards practice is highly unbecoming, especially since it has no source of knowledge which cannot also be acquired by means of empirical observation. The man of science would of course investigate the sources more thoroughly and purposefully than the common man would, but this does not change the fact that both are observing the same realities through the same senses. In the past, scholars and philosophers have often considered the *vulgus profanum*—that is, the common people—to be below them. The aristocratic artists often considered themselves to be "Übermenschen," looking down upon the common herd, and the same can be said of many men of science. They often speak as if they possess some additional sense with which to observe yet another world—one invisible to the common man. Thus, while the masses have to be content with sensual observations, with faith, and with how things appear to them, they alone supposedly possess speculative reason and the ability to contemplate findings, thereby elevating themselves to the level of *gnosis*, in which they acquire knowledge of ideas of which others can only remain ignorant. And if such contemplation turns out to be not acquirable through normal epistemic methods, they fabricate an artificial and elevated method of knowledge acquisition. But for science, just as for religion and the arts, this has always been a most dangerous course which can only lead to a rude awakening and deep disappointment.

Regardless of how sophisticated and broad scientific investigation becomes, it never sees a world not visible to everyone and it never acquires a sense not also possessed by the common man. We are not able to investigate anything which is not part of that which creation offers to our consciousness. And nothing can become our knowledge unless it has been first observed by us. That which we cannot observe and that which does not enter our consciousness can obviously not be studied by us. We even cannot pronounce judgment with regard to its non-existence. This fact all Christian scientists realize, as they unanimously maintain that all knowledge starts with observation. They would not have a problem with Kant's proposition that "knowledge without sight is empty."

But while scientists must caution against the implicit idea that they possess superior senses that the common people don't, they should also on the other hand remain cautious against any school which arbitrarily limits the trustworthiness of empirical observation. In the normal course of life, we instinctively assume that we have absolute certainty not only of that which we can see and hear but also of all things to which our consciousness bears witness. We know that there exists a visible world outside of us and that in addition to the physical or visible world there also exists a world of truth, goodness, and beauty. That is integral to our self-consciousness—a kind of immediate knowledge. We are not mere animals, but people who are rational, moral, religious, and aesthetic beings. The realization of truth, goodness, and beauty is integral to our nature. The distinctions between truth and falsehood, good and evil, justice and injustice, godlessness and godliness are to our consciousness just as evident as the distinctions between light and darkness, day and night, sweet and sour, sound and silence, value and loss, and pleasant and unpleasant. In order to erase these realizations, we would have to completely destroy human nature. Every human being instinctively has these realizations. Unconsciously, this underlies all of our thoughts and actions and all of our desires and feelings. Upon this realization the family, society, state, religion, morality, and law—in fact, the entire history and structure of human society—are built. And it is from here that science also needs to proceed.

Just as much as speculative rationalism, perceptual realism can also be resisted, as it arbitrarily questions the truthfulness and certainty of observation, and it proceeds from the idea that through observation, to the exclusion of philosophical presuppositions, impressions are redirected towards our senses. It completely disregards the fact that making observations through the senses is, qualitatively speaking, just as much as rational thought, a psychologically complex activity. It disregards the fact that psychological phenomena form an independent reality which is, in practice, for virtually all people just as much a source of knowledge as natural phenomena are. It fails to take into account that the psychological realm is not merely a process of observation and thought but contains within itself the key to unlocking the world of ideas, which is as real and undeniable as the world we see with our eyes and touch with our hands. Therefore, it proposes a collision course with reality and life, with the facts of religion and morality which it does not explain but seeks to destroy, or at least reduce to complete arbitrariness.

Principle, presupposition, and foundation are therefore in the final instance the witnesses of our self-consciousness. Therein lies the indestructible realization of the existence of a world both in us and outside of us, of the soul and the body, of spirit and matter, of visible and invisible things.[3] Of course, there is no dualism between these two worlds. They are both realities that we come to know through the one and undivided self-consciousness. Soul and body are intrinsically related, and invisible realities are revealed through visible ones. We do not observe the physical world apart from a psychological activity, as it is the soul of man which observes through his eyes and hears through his ears. And because the human soul is indeed here the true object and the senses but only the means, he can interpret and understand the nature and purpose of the things he observes. How invisible things manifest in visible things we do not know. That which comes to us externally is, physically speaking, nothing other than vibrations of air

---

[3] Dr. Bruining rightly remarks in an article in *Teyler's Theological Journal* that "the acknowledgment of the reality of the outside world is not a product of rational thought, which proceeds from conceptualization to the acknowledgment of external causes. We cannot describe the psychological process as such. But the representation comes to us with a measure of objectivity, that is, as a representation of something outside of us. And the difference between realism and idealism is therefore not that idealism remains stuck in the representation to which realism attaches something concrete. On the contrary, realism takes the representation as it represents itself, whereas idealism denies its original character." The same can be said with regard to psychological, religious, moral, and aesthetic phenomena: they include the reality of the world of invisible things—the world of ideas. He who denies the latter necessarily has to deny the former also.

and ether, which stimulate our senses.[4] The way in which these physical phenomena become signs and carriers of thought through our observation we do not know. But this mystery does not invalidate the facts. By means of this, we discover the reality of design in the world, laws in nature, order in the universe, beauty in creation, as well as love and faithfulness in the heart. From all sides, these things encroach upon our self-consciousness. They come to us through different means: through our eyes and ears, through observation and thought, through authority and reason, through examination and tradition. They reflect back, not only upon the visible world which surrounds us but also upon the world of ideas, which is revealed to us through the rational and moral nature of our self-consciousness. We are not merely indifferent spectators, but we appreciate and judge, approve and disapprove, admire and loathe, love and hate. We also, therefore, distinguish between true and false and accordingly judge the propositions we encounter, thoughtfully process them, and in science and scholarship aim for the truth.

For this very reason, scientific knowledge is not at odds with empirical observation and practical experience built

---

[4] Bavinck's reference to ether shows that he was keeping up with the leading scientific theories of his time. The ether theory perhaps began with Isaac Newton. It has since been abandoned.—Ed.

thereupon. But it is rather based thereupon and proceeds from it, while attempting to, by means of thorough investigation, elicit, explain, and expand it. As Kaftan puts it: "Expanding and explaining normal knowledge is the purpose of science."[5] All empirical knowledge is

---

[5] *Die Wahrheit der christlichen Religion* (Basel, 1889), 319. Compare also the statement of Spencer in his *First Principles*, 5th edition, 18: "What is science? To see the absurdity of the prejudice against it, we need only remark that science is simply a higher development of common knowledge; and that if science is repudiated, all knowledge must be repudiated along with it. The extremist bigot will not suspect any harm in the observation, that the sun rises earlier and sets later in the summer than in the winter, but will rather consider such an observation as a useful aid in fulfilling the duties of life. Well, astronomy is an organized body of similar observation, made with greater nicety, extended to a larger number of objects and so analyzed as to disclose the real arrangement of the heavens, and to dispel our false conceptions of them. That iron will rust in winter, that wood will burn, that long-kept viands become putrid, the most timid sectarian will teach them, without alarm, as things useful to be known. But these are chemical truths: chemistry is a systematic collection of such facts, ascertained with precision, and so classified and generalized as to enable us to say with certainty, concerning each simple or compound substance, what change will occur in it under given conditions. And thus it is with all the sciences. They severely germinate out of the experience of daily life; insensibly as they grow, they draw in remoter, more numerous, and more complex experiences; and among these, they ascertain laws of dependence like those which make up our knowledge of the most familiar objects. Nowhere is it possible to draw a line and say: here science begins."

taken into account by scientific investigation. We have, through practical experience, come to realize the reality not only of the visible and natural phenomena which surround us but also of the invisible and supernatural world, of which we as rational and moral beings are the citizenry. This world is also the object of scientific investigation, and not for the purpose of proving or disproving its existence, but to come to the knowledge of its nature and its laws. Therefore, limiting the scope of science is, to my mind, highly suspect. Nonetheless, from the perspective of the subject—that is, the human investigator—there are certainly limits to be placed upon science. Our knowledge is always limited and incomplete, our life is short, and our energy is swiftly exhausted. The absolute philosophy that believes in a kind of gradual progress through world history culminating in the establishment of a heavenly kingdom here on earth is a chiliast dream. That we only know in part will always remain the confession of all people here on earth. But it nonetheless remains impossible to draw a clear line between the world of phenomena in which hard sciences operate and the *terra incognita* outside of that world. This is because it cannot be shown why the things outside of the circle of exact sciences should be considered unknowable. Is it because they supposedly do not exist? If so, how would we know where to draw the line? Is it because although they do exist, they are naturally unknowable? If so, then they would be unthinkable and consequently non-existent. Is it because they do exist and are knowable, but our knowledge is not equipped to ascend to their level? If so, then we would have to accept a very strange view of knowability since this would make a host of exact, existent, knowable, and very important things for us unknowable. Kant and others answered these propositions by arguing that God has created us in such a way, that it is not in theoretical knowledge but in moral action that the chief end of man is situated. But such a response dodges the true issue. The question is, after all, why we have been epistemically structured in such a way that we cannot know the things that we would love to know. The quest for truth is, after all, by no means sinful, and truth is not a lesser good than holiness or glory.

What is more, however, is that while we can theoretically try to limit the scope of science, nobody in practice adheres to those limits. Every human being has an innate metaphysical desire. It was with questions regarding the deepest issues of life and the nature, cause, and purpose of all things that science started with the Greeks, and these are the universal motivations behind science. What we long for and need for our lives is a worldview that satisfies both our mind and our soul. Such a worldview cannot be built by natural phenomena alone but is also based upon those realities which we acquire through internal experience. It must provide a coherent unity to all of our thought and action, reconcile knowledge and faith, and establish peace between our mind and heart. We believe this peace is possible, and we strive towards it because truth cannot be in opposition to itself since there is but one human spirit, one world, and one God. As far off as that ideal still may be, the chief end of science is always knowledge of pure, unadulterated truth. If knowledge will never become understanding, how will we ever find God? But knowledge is something different and something higher than understanding; it does not exclude mystery and adoration. All science is the interpretation of divine thought as manifested in divine works. False science leads us away from God, while true science leads to increased knowledge of Him. In Him alone, who is Himself truth, we find rest, both for our mind and our heart. As Augustine says: "For rest lies in entirety—that is, in full perfection—but in part there is toil."[6]

The Natural Sciences

Science, in general, therefore has the entire cosmos as its object and the systematic knowledge thereof as its purpose. It would only be complete and achieve its goal when we come to knowledge of all reality as a whole in terms of its final cause and purpose, as well as its essence and inherent relationships. Science leads to philosophy, just as it has its historical

---

[6] Augustine, *The City of God*, Book XI, chapter 31.

origins in philosophy. But as its investigation develops further and evolves into reflection, science is split into a wide variety of fields. The whole precedes the parts, which, as members of the organism of science, gradually grew and developed out of the whole. And this process of differentiation continues even today. Currently, science has split into so many different groups and fields that her intrinsic unity is often forgotten with her practitioners preoccupied with detail-studies and with universities falling apart into a variety of vocational schools. Thankfully, the dangers of overspecialization have been recognized in recent years, and the desire for the *vinculum scientiarum* and the study of philosophy has been emphatically revived.

As long as this unity is remembered, the splitting of science into a wide variety of fields can be considered to be a most healthy development. The field of research is, after all, so incredibly broad, that a division of labor is inescapable. But it must always be remembered that every field of scientific research, while standing in direct relation to the whole, is a distinct and particular application thereof. And this differentiation is made in accordance with the object of study. The world is one whole and yet immeasurably diverse. Matter and spirit, nature and history, human and animal, soul and body, Church and state, family and society, trade and industry: they are all interrelated, but also reciprocally distinct, each with its own nature and characteristics, as well as its own life and laws. This unity in diversity needs to be acknowledged by all fields of science. At the university, it is important that both the unity as well as the uniqueness and independence of the sciences are cultivated. Then alone can it claim to be a *universitas scientiarum*. Both pantheistic fusion and deistic disintegration are to be avoided.

It is also therefore evident that there is not one single normative method for all sciences. Already in terms of the talents and tact of the researcher, every particular science posits its own unique demands. Some are gifted to excel in mathematics or biology, some in terms of legal or literary science, while some are best equipped for historiography and others for philosophy. Not everyone is equally suited for all fields. There must be a direct relationship between the subject and the object. As the arts form a unified whole and yet every type of art has its own distinct characteristics and demands, so the unity of all sciences does not preclude that every field of study shares certain characteristics with all others.

If this is so, then it is obvious that research methods would differ with regard to and in accordance with the nature of the object of research, as would the foundations of the investigation as well as the surety of the results. There are not only vast differences concerning the so-called natural sciences and humanities in this but also between the various natural sciences themselves. It has to be emphasized once again that all sciences, even those which study natural phenomena, are fundamentally based upon metaphysical presuppositions and proceed from pre-theoretical commitments to the truth of specific axioms as a point of departure. There is, for example, no science possible without an uncritical faith in the reliability of the senses, a faith in the objective existence of the world, a faith in the existence of a rational order in that world, and a faith in the existence of a consistent logic by which that order can be interpreted. While this is not the place to delve deeper into this aspect, I would like to note that there exists a large difference between the various fields of natural science and that they cannot all be based on a single model. Since the days of Kepler and Newton, scientists have been able to cultivate astronomy by means of a mathematical model, and this has been partially achieved also for physics, chemistry, and even physiology. Jealous of the kind of certainty achieved in these fields, other fields of science also strove to achieve the same kind of mathematical truth. There is, if men like Oken are to be believed, only one absolute certainty—mathematical certainty, or as Du Bois-Reymond calls it—no knowledge apart from the physical-mathematical.

Therefore, the same requirement is also placed before various other sciences, such as biology, to explain and cast its findings in a mechanical-chemical fashion. But even if this demand—that all natural phenomena are to be explained in a mechanical manner—were to be maintained, then there still arises among scientists a dispute regarding the distinction and limits of the respective sciences. With organic beings, the relationships are, after all, so complex and there are so many forces at play, that everything cannot be simply explained by using simple formulae such as the biogenetic law or natural selection. Haeckel, for example, noted the role of philosophical presuppositions in the interpretation of the findings of experience. In his lecture on "The Current Theory of Evolution in Relation to Science as a Whole," delivered in Stuttgart in 1878, he acknowledged that his teachings regarding the origins and evolution of organic beings are experimental and unproven. After all, biology is, by its very nature, a historical and philosophical natural science. Thus, even if an exact mathematical standard of proof were, in principle, to be maintained for all sciences, it would not be practically applicable for most of biology's field of study. Rather than the exact mathematical method, the historical and philosophical method would be much more appropriate for this field. Later, Haeckel indeed also advocated for a monist philosophy, which is itself not based upon facts but upon his own subjective convictions.

But there are others who protest mixing science and philosophy. Bastian, for example, in a time where induction and experiment are prevalent, reproves Haeckel for granting any influence to theory and accuses him of violating the most sacred principles of science. Virchow makes a sharp distinction between the speculative terrain of natural sciences and the factual terrain, counting descent theory among the latter. Du Bois-Reymond opposed this same confusion, drawing sharp borderlines for natural science, arguing that there are no less than seven world wonders which cannot be explained by mechanical means. Haeckel's *Weltradsel* was therefore also later heavily criticized, not only by theologians and philosophers but also by natural scientists. And while Haeckel advocates a return to the philosophy of Spinoza, other scientists now side themselves with Leibniz. In innumerable circles, the mechanical explanation of the world is now making way for organic, teleologic, and even theistic explanations. With this in mind, it can hardly be denied that science is also influenced by worldview and philosophy, and consequently also faith or unbelief.[7] While science had, during the

---

[7] Medical science is no different. In fact, here it is even more evident since it is not based upon scientific principles but practical experience. The faculty of medicine now consists of a number of fields which actually properly belong with the faculty of natural science, but which are for practical reasons absorbed by the faculty of medicine so as to enable the training of doctors. But it has a distinctly empirical character, despite being, throughout its history, guided by theories. A whole series of medical systems have historically arisen and fallen again. So it was in Greece, in the Middle Ages, and in the modern era. The contemporary systems are, interestingly, also marked by the return to

nineteenth century, first come under the spell of Hegel and Schelling, who guided it in a particular direction, and while it would later be shaped by Darwinism and materialism, there is currently a marked return to the philosophy of Leibniz. And this was to be expected, of course. Arts, religion, politics, society, law, and morals are always impacted by the spirit of the age—and science is no exception to this rule. Even scientists are men of their time and cannot liberate themselves from their contexts. This is neither possible when we are observing and constituting phenomena, nor in particular when it comes to the application of our findings and the search for the laws which regulate observed phenomena. Analysis by itself is insufficient for science, and it must continually be amended and supplemented by synthesis. Goethe argues that no analysis can be done without synthesis. A pile of sand cannot be analyzed, he claims, since it consists of a variety of elements. You take sand or gold and wash it by means of analysis so that the lightest parts drift away and only the heaviest parts remain. Only by utilizing both analysis and synthesis can science flourish. So Goethe argues in his *Das Wesen der Wissenschaft*, page 21.

---

ancient principles. The newer means of healing utilizing baths, air, music, sunbathing massages, hypnosis, gymnastics, etc., are all a revival of ancient methods. Some medical scholars therefore rightly advocate the need for a history of medicine.

Practicing science therefore not only requires sharp observation, clarity of mind, diligence, a good method, and precise investigation, but also a creative imagination, genial intuition, and surprising divination. These insights have not always been methodically produced. They have often been the result of geniuses thinking outside the box. The progress of science is furthermore not limited to purely experimental research—although this of course forms a most integral part thereof—but also the result of strokes of genius. Thousands had already observed an apple fall from a tree, but it took the genius of Newton to discover the law of gravity. At first, these insights are nothing other than hypotheses, but these hypotheses are proven to be true and even become unmissable for science itself, leading to further research and clarifying a host of phenomena. Once they are confirmed by further observation, they become theory and law. But they must also, however dearly they may be held, immediately be discarded if disproven by subsequent investigation. There can be no debate regarding this truth. Hypotheses are only useful as long as they serve to clarify the facts. But they are sadly often presented, even if they still only have a preliminary character, as the sure and set results of science by a multitude of scientists, even after they have long been proven to be untenable. History offers us ample examples where so-called irrefutable scientific facts are used against religion, only to be soon thereafter discarded due to subsequent results. Even the most widely held natural laws are not indubitable. The recently discovered element of radium greatly challenges the law regarding the maintenance of labor potential and no one knows—so it has been written in light of this recent discovery—what the fate will be of the formerly established laws of iron, which for the greatest part of the nineteenth century had been accepted as foundational.

This nonetheless evidences that the sciences can in no way be separated from the philosophy, the impact of subjectivity, or the worldview of the researcher. Modesty and a love of truth are therefore virtues most appropriate to scientists. In mathematics, chemistry, and anatomy, the differences in worldview may only play a minor role, but in the fields of geology, paleontology, biology, and anthropology, the difference between faith and unbelief is decisive.

The Humanities

This is even more true for the humanities. However, it must be noted that the sharp distinction between the humanities and natural sciences is itself not above suspicion. After all, natural sciences also work with propositions regarding non-visible realities underlying natural phenomena and operate by means of the use of reason. Likewise, the humanities are not only built upon philosophical constructions and rational ideas but also work with observable artistic and literary works, as well as historical and existing institutions. But the distinction is what it is, and so the so-called humanities are nowadays acknowledged as a distinct branch of knowledge. However, many remain ignorant of their place in the world of science. It is self-evident, after all, that if the methods of natural science are the only true scientific ones, the humanities have to occupy a lower position and have to be prescribed by the natural sciences. After all, if Comte is to be believed, the humanities continue to remain stuck in the theological or metaphysical phase. While he who refuses to acknowledge God as the source of right and law can still acknowledge the moral instincts of our human nature which underlie the humanities, once all theology and metaphysics are removed from the equation, the humanities would supposedly also either proceed to the positivist phase or willingly dissolve themselves. But naturally, there are many who rightly oppose such a development because this would imply nothing less than the complete absorption of the humanities into the natural sciences. The proposal has consequently been made by the likes of Windelband, to maintain the humanities alongside the natural sciences as a kind of "historical study."

Such a distinction needs to be credited for acknowledging the difference between nature and history and between the empirical and the historical method, as such a distinction is vital for science itself. But this distinction is still incorrect. Firstly, because the border between natural science and historiography can only be arbitrarily drawn. Windelband claims that they are formally distinct in that science seeks to discover general laws, while history is preoccupied with particular facts. Neither aims at apodictic judgments and for the one nomothetic thinking is required, while the other requires an idiographic approach. But even he must admit that the same fields, such as geology and astronomy, can often be characterized by both approaches. Every field of science has both a systematic and a historical element. Natural sciences can, in terms of geology, paleontology, and geography, not operate without the historical method, while historiography itself does not limit itself to particular facts, but looks for the ideas and causes behind those facts.

Additionally, such a distinction would mean that psychology would be completely absorbed by the natural sciences, while religion, ethics, law, and art would be reduced to historical studies. This would amount to an injustice towards psychology since although there is an undeniable relationship between psychological and physical realities, they are most certainly very distinct. This profound distinction would have to be completely ignored for psychology to be absorbed by natural science. But if this distinction is not acknowledged in terms of psychology, it can of course not be upheld when it comes to the categorization of subjects that occupy themselves with religion, ethics, arts, and literature. If our opponents were to maintain that this distinction is not based upon the nature of the respective objects of study, but rather on whether the empirical or historical method is followed in terms of that study, then they would disregard not only the aforementioned reply—namely that the methodical distinction is not so clear-cut—but also the fact that the object of study is itself decisive in terms of the method of investigation it requires.

But in the third place, an even more serious objection to this distinction lies therein that if the fields of religion, ethics, and law are limited to the historical method, they would lose their normative character. This would mean that while the natural sciences would be allowed to trace laws and apply the nomothetic approach, Windelband's position would limit the former fields to the study of religious, ethical, and legal phenomena, and be left with the mere objective of describing the richness of human life as this has historically manifested in religion, ethics, law, language, and arts. Of course, this would mean losing all authority to make any epistemic or axiological claims, maintaining a wholly subjective character at best. Faith and unbelief, godliness and godlessness, love and hate, justice and injustice, good and evil, and truth and deception would all have an equal right to exist as historical phenomena. No objective standard remains. All these fields of knowledge would not retain the right to make any claims regarding what constitutes true religion, ethics, or law, but only what had historically been accepted as such.

But, in conclusion, it must be maintained that these fields cannot be content with having a merely descriptive character. That is perhaps desired by some, but it is completely impractical. Everyone expects these sciences to explain to us what true and normative religion, ethics, and law are. The nature of man is such, that this desire and expectation on his part is inescapable. According to the classical conception thereof, philosophy is intrinsically tied to wisdom, for example. But even if there were no such expectation on the part of man, these sciences would still not be able to limit themselves to such demands—for science and knowledge itself pertains to the truth. Phenomena are not enough, since science itself desires norms, laws, and authority. This fact is also evident when we observe the effects of the position of those who desire to reduce all science to merely having either a positivist or historiographical nature. In abandoning an absolute standard for judging good and evil, scholars attempt to utilize statistics and history to evaluate what would in the future be regarded as normative in terms of truth, law, and ethics. "The greatest happiness for the greatest number" becomes the sole norm in religion, morality, logic, and aesthetics. In itself, everything is a private matter—a matter of either taste and passion, or else of character and education.

But because this would lead to licentious arbitrariness, individualism needs to be subdued by socialism. Science, represented by an Areopagus of scholars, must therefore prescribe to everyone, on the basis of their own historical and statistical analysis, what constitutes truth. They have the highest authority. In earlier times, the Church and the state, religion, and the clergy governed humanity; but now it is the turn of science to act as the benefactress of the nations and redeemer of mankind. It must now authoritatively proclaim the dogmas and norms which govern all of human life. Based on historical and statistical analysis, scientists must proclaim whether monotheism or polytheism, truth or lies, marriage or debauchery is to be preferred. The only force, Clavel proclaims, which has the privilege of demanding faith and obedience, is science. It must prescribe, on the basis of facts, what is good for the family, the nation, and humanity as a whole. If society is benefited more from lies than from truth, these two must swap places—because mankind does not exist for the sake of truth, but truth for the sake of mankind, from whom and through whom it exists. The timelessness of moral principles consists only in becoming timeless by the hand of man. And, in order to ensure obedience to dictates, the state has to enforce it by means of violence.

This is the result of the application of positivism to the humanities, which leads not only to undermining the very foundations of human life, but also to a type of scientific hierarchy, which seriously threatens our liberties. And this hierarchy is even more unbearable given its net result of arbitrariness and anarchy. It is after all, easy to see how the positivist-empirical method is completely inapplicable to the humanities. Even with regard to natural science, it proves itself insufficient because it is only by virtue of combination, analysis, and synthesis can any study claim to be scientific. But concerning the humanities, it is much worse, since its application leads to the complete destruction of this field. In principle, this is acknowledged by all those who at least still maintain the distinction between the empirical and historical methods. But if a hard distinction between these two methods is maintained, then the humanities can never acquire any level of certainty, which is then reserved for the natural sciences. History, after all, always rests upon fallible, human witness, which ultimately needs to be accepted upon faith and therefore can never acquire mathematical certainty. And with this, history becomes a field not governed by natural laws, but where personal preference is decisive. It is acknowledged that some historians also apply the empirical method and strive towards discovering set natural laws, but this is said to lead to bad historiography. It is held that the laws that man had previously regarded as the fruits of religion, ethics, arts, and the historical development of the state and society, are not more than mere typical social regularities. The scientific nature of historiography itself is doubted and regarded as unsuitable to be taught even at school.

The independence of the humanities is only maintained if we acknowledge its foundation as our self-conscious realization of truthful realities, morality, and law. In a certain sense, even the objects of study in the natural sciences are, to us, only available in the form of representations of our own self-consciousness. We cannot ever view the world outside of us apart from our own self-consciousness. But, as was also remarked earlier, there is still an important methodological distinction. While the natural sciences, by means of these representations, always strive toward knowledge of the outside world, the humanities focus on "unmediated experience, which is shaped by the interaction of objects with observing and active subjects," to borrow the words of Wundt. For the humanities, the objects represented are the movements of the subject and their context, which they strive to explain in terms of their origin and essence. This does not mean that the humanities are nothing more than a consciousness-science, and therefore a subfield of psychology. Because even if, as with all the sciences, their roots lie in the soul, they strive towards a knowledge of reality that objectively exists but can only be psychologically observed. In philology, history, and philosophy, as well as in law, political science, and sociology, the object of study is always man in terms of his internal, invisible, and spiritual side. This is not confined to the study of what man is as an individual, but also—just as with medical science—what he is both socially and in relation to the family and the state. All these sciences have not only a historical, but also a systematic nature and aim. But they would not be able to proceed with their task without presupposing the truth that human nature is a constant given. Philology is not possible without the presupposition that there is a certain *logos* to language. History cannot be practiced without the presupposition that all events are guided by an overarching idea and are teleologically directed toward a given purpose. Psychology's right to an independent existence can only be maintained upon the presupposition that psychological phenomena radically differ from physical phenomena. Ethics and aesthetics lose their scientific character once the norms of good and evil, and beauty and non-beauty are discarded. And legal theory loses its right to exist the moment we cease to acknowledge a standard of justice with which legal systems can be tested.

These fields are not speculative sciences, as language and morals, justice and law, and state and society are all founded upon *a priori* principles. Nonetheless, they are all bound to the psychological realm in which all these phenomena reveal themselves. Legal theorists have the right to investigate existing legal systems and therein find the material of their object of study. So it is with all the humanities: in a certain sense, they are positivistic, that is, they find their object of study in the physical world. Even philosophy would lose itself in vain speculation had it not taken the physical world into account. But in order to come to knowledge and to judge the world which exists outside of us, we need to proceed from the witness of our own consciousness, that is, our soul's realization of reality and subsequent propositions. For the humanities, there are no other sources of knowledge than empirical studies upon which the psychological realm is built. If they were to disregard this, however, they would condemn themselves to utter fruitlessness and descend into a fatal dichotomy between life and study. The family, the state, society, language, law, and ethics are built upon psychological self-consciousness.

This is not to say that science ought to simply uncritically embrace the status quo, of course. But in order to produce a pure and truthful criticism of it, science needs to be in possession of set standards from which to proceed. This is provided through the witness of our own consciousness. Herein every human being, either willingly or unwillingly, finds the acknowledgment of the existence of truth, goodness, and beauty which cannot be deduced from empirical realities. Every human being is a citizen of not only the natural realm but also of the moral order of creation as a rational and moral being—and this is a citizenship we cannot escape. Therein lies the essence, the greatness, and the glory of mankind. The more we become aware of this higher nature of man, the more we are, like Kant, filled with amazement thereof, and the merits of every objection against presupposing this reality melts away. Since if we were not to believe in ourselves in this regard, what reasons would we have to accept the witness of our self-consciousness when it comes to perceiving the world around us? In this most intimate self-realization of the soul, in our deepest convictions, in the royalty of human nature rests the majesty of the subject of our investigation: the foundation upon which all sciences, but in particular the humanities, rest. Science can only be of service to mankind, not in the place of, but next to religion, as long as it recognizes the rational and moral nature of man and builds upon the faith therein.

Theology As Science

The last field of study worth mentioning is theology, where all the aforementioned facts are even more evident. Under the influence of Kant's epistemic critique and due to a fear of modern science, many have made the most destructive concessions when it comes to theology's place among the sciences. They have conceded that no knowledge of God is possible and that therefore theology as such cannot be considered a science. Consequently, they have advocated transforming the faculty of theology into a faculty of religious studies and have achieved success by means of the 1876 Dutch law regarding higher education. The proponents of this position figured that they had preserved the scientific status of theology by virtue of shifting its object of study from God to religion as a socio-historical phenomenon. After all, the significance and importance of religion as a historical phenomenon cannot be denied by anyone.

This is of course true, but the question remains whether religious studies is thereby justified as being an independent faculty. Judging by the tone by which so-called progressive scholars nowadays often address and discuss this new field of science and the general attitude they have towards it; it cannot be said that this shift has indeed benefited or advanced the reputation of this field. Many men of science may of course approve of professional theologians opposing the truths of the Christian faith, but this in essence violates the rights of the field of religious studies. While it is true that the history of religion itself garners much scholarly interest, the moment historical religion is proposed as relevant for today, interest makes way for apathy, and even at times for loathing. Modern religion and theology in reality serve the scientist just as little as they do the common man. The scientific reputation of theology has therefore been damaged by its metamorphosis into religious studies.

This is also not surprising, as the transition itself has been half-hearted, which has led to criticism from both the left and the right. In the combination of subjects categorized under theology by the 1876 law, there lies ample proof of this, because it is a mixture of subjects from the old faculty of theology and the new faculty of religious studies. This confusion is further amplified by the fact that the faculty wants to promote a new science under an old banner— the new faculty is one focused on religious studies and desires to be as such, but still retains the name of theology. The same half-heartedness is also evident in the character and purpose of religious studies itself. After all, it is not meant to be only limited to the study of the phenomenon of religion but also desires to acquire knowledge of the essence and origin of religion. But in starting with the history of religion, it eventually leads to dogmatics, to the philosophy of religion, and to ethics. But according to the contemporary conception of science, as we have noted, there is only room for the empirical, and maybe also for the historical method. Many argue that dogmatics, which proposes the essence and truth of religion, cannot be considered scientific at all. If religious studies were to attempt this, they would immediately surrender their scientific status, which they sought to preserve by means of the aforementioned metamorphosis, because, through purely historical and empirical *viae,* one can never come to a concrete religious doctrine. If religious studies lead to this, then it means that they are not only objectively studying religion as a phenomenon but are instead advocating a certain appreciation of that phenomenon. But if any study limits itself to investigating religion as a historical phenomenon, then it would be better suited to the faculty of literary science. If theology desires to remain an independent faculty, then the foundation of that desire must be the conviction that its object of study is much more than merely a historical phenomenon. It, after all, proceeds from the presupposition that religion is an objective truth—that is, not the mere product of human imagination or a psychological manifestation, but a necessary given in human nature and a virtue pertaining to the essence of man—and therefore has a right to an independent existence as faculty.

This presupposition is of such great significance and so rich in content that there remains no reason for liberal theologians to boast of their so-called scientific objectivity, or to look down upon orthodox theologians as men caught up in their own dogmas. This is because this presupposition is central to and inescapable for all scientific scholarship. If religion constitutes an objective truth, then it naturally follows that not all religions of mankind can be considered equally true. Because religions—as opposed to languages, for example—naturally stand in competition to one another, in that what one regards as truth the other regards as falsehood, and consequently they necessarily condemn one another. In contradistinction to its proclaimed tolerance, liberal theology is no exception to the rule. They might claim that all religions share a common origin, that none of them possess the full truth, and that ultimately it is not doctrine but living right that matters, but in practice, these people fight against all other religions with the same vigor with which the respective religions fight one another. And this is certainly inescapable since if any man is convinced of the truth of his own confession, he cannot simply stand in apathy towards contrasting confessions. This is because in religion we always deal with what man regards as the chief end of his existence, and its character is such that it cannot ever be neutral. Orthodoxy and modernism cannot be simultaneously true. If the first is true, the second is false, and vice versa. Modernist theology therefore not only also presupposes that religion, in general, constitutes an objective truth, but that it also adheres to a specific religious conviction that constitutes its own religious confession. After all, it generally confesses that those religious convictions are truthful and are universally manifested and that it has found its greatest and purest expression in Christianity—first in the Reformation, and now finally in liberal theology. Whether or not modernist theology produces a concrete confession of faith, whether it forms an ecclesiastical structure or cult changes nothing regarding this reality. Even if it, in accordance with romanticist notions, only exists in sentiment independent from all symbols and institutions—something which would of course not be claimed by any modernist theologian and something which is practically impossible anyway—it would still represent a distinct religion. It, after all, not only believes in the truthfulness of religion in general but is also convinced that the conception of religion it adheres to is the true one and that all other forms of religion are deficient and impure.

But also contained in the presupposition upon which the faculty of religious studies is built, there is something of even greater significance. If we are to seriously consider the contents of our confession, we would have to unequivocally proclaim that the belief in the objective truth of religion also entails the belief in the existence of a personal God. Because it is after all undeniable that if God does not exist, religion, or the service and worship of God, is the greatest foolishness, but if religion is in any way truthful, then the existence of God must be assumed. Theology, understood to be knowledge of God, is the very heart of religion. If religious studies desire to be not purely empirical and historical—in which case they would have to be classed as literary science— but if they also desire to acquire knowledge of true religion through empirical and historical means, then they have to presuppose the truth of religion and, of necessity, thereby also the existence of God. But this acknowledgment of the existence of God intrinsic to the acceptance of truthfulness in religion is in turn also inseparable from the belief in the knowability of God, since an unknowable God is, in practice, to us men, a non-existent God. And in the end, if God is acknowledged to be knowable, albeit in a very limited manner, then it follows that He has revealed Himself to us, because that which we cannot observe we cannot know, and that which we cannot know we cannot love or serve. The modern faculty of religious studies which is founded upon the presupposition of the truthfulness of religion therefore also presupposes the revelation and knowability of God. In other words, it is still caught up in metaphysics, having left behind the terrain of the supernatural only partially. In fact, naturalism and religion are irreconcilable. All religion is supernatural and presupposes that God transcends the world and is essentially distinct from the world, but that He enters the world in order to reveal Himself. Praying for a pure heart, Pierson rightly claimed, is equally supernatural as praying for the healing of a sick person. Formally there is therefore no difference between orthodox and liberal believers. There is no room for religious studies if God does not exist, is not knowable, and has not revealed Himself. It is therefore short-sighted and deceptive to say to another:

> With you it is dogmatism, with me it is science. You are prejudiced and biased, but I objectively approach my research and accept nothing that cannot be

proven. While I also hold certain presuppositions, you hold onto yours despite the results of scientific investigation, while I only employ them as hypotheses which I discard once they have been scientifically disproven.

If the presuppositions are merely hypotheses that have no relation to religious convictions, then the orthodox believers would just as willingly sacrifice them as would the liberals. But of course, neither would simply do so the moment someone happens to challenge them through scholarship. Both would weigh and judge said scholarship. He who investigates the history of science, especially of the nineteenth century, would eventually become immune to excitement upon reading any report and become gradually more and more convinced of its human errors and fallibility. But wherever true and genuine science is found, the orthodox Christian would embrace it just as much as the liberal would. There is no one who does not acknowledge and appreciate the scientific discoveries and breakthroughs of the past century. But not a single man of science considers himself irrevocably bound by conscience to hypotheses.

But it is radically different when it comes to the presuppositions upon which scientific investigation is built, as these are not mere hypotheses, but the deepest convictions inherent to the human soul which arise from our very humanity. These pre-theoretical commitments cannot be discarded by virtue of the outcome of scientific investigation. He who confesses with Asaph, "Whom do I have in heaven but You? And earth has nothing I desire besides You," cannot simultaneously claim that this faith is merely a hypothesis that he discards as soon as science shows it to be untenable. If he were to speak like this, he would prove himself to be not a true believer but a hypocrite. In this regard, there is no difference between liberals and conservatives or between Roman Catholics and Protestants. All who have high regard for religion and look to God for their salvation, cannot remain neutral with regard to the claims promoted by the science of the day. But we should proclaim with one voice that those most sacred and deepest convictions of ours are things that science can never rob us of. It must stay away from these, as they fall outside of its domain. And if it dared to do so it would extend itself beyond its own confines and reveal itself to be a false science. Thousands of scholars may at any given time claim that my faith is foolishness, but over and against the science of the *zeitgeist* I call upon the science of the ages.

This is the language of faith, and this is the way all those speak who regard religion as objectively true. This does not, of course, mean that people like us are not open to change or to being convinced by new findings. Even if it is the rule for people to die in the religion they were brought up with, many are converted by means of missions, and believers often transition from one denomination to another. Roman Catholics become Protestants and vice versa; and modernists now see their adherence strengthened by converts from orthodox Christianity. But what is the nature of these conversions? Is this the same as when a scientist forsakes a hypothesis when it is disproven? No one would claim this. If a Roman Catholic becomes Protestant, or a modernist becomes orthodox, then such a transition, assuming that it is genuine, is the result of a religious and moral crisis that took place in the depths of the human soul. The Christian, guided by Scripture, even confesses that no one who is not regenerated by God can come to faith in Christ. The natural man does not understand that which is revealed by the Holy Spirit. In order to see the kingdom of heaven, one needs to be born again through water and Spirit, and whosoever later leaves the Church proves thereby that he has never truly been a member thereof. The nature of such religious transitions evidence that they are wholly different from those in science, where the testing of hypotheses has nothing to do with moral or religious changes which bring about a confessional transition. Everyone would like to rid himself of prejudice and become better informed, but no truly religious person would consider his own theological and moral convictions to be prejudices. After all, if he embraces these in his soul, he could never do so. After all, for the sake of reconciliation with God, he not only is willing to sacrifice his scientific status but even his possessions and his very life. It is upon religion that the well-being of man depends. Losing one's soul means losing everything.

3

Revelation

Formally speaking, the believer's approach towards scientific investigation is therefore no different than that of non-believers. He who believes in the existence, revelation, and knowability of God must hold, with heart and mind, that faith and science should always be in harmony with each other. He must strive towards a holistic worldview in which there is not only room for science but also religion. Yet the formal agreement with the approach of the unbeliever is also necessarily accompanied by a material difference. The question which divides religions and confessions is this: Where is the revelation of God to be found from which we can know Him? In other words, what is the source of religion?

In earlier centuries men had been prone to view all of creation as the revelation of God however, since the eighteenth century, the content of this revelation has been increasingly limited. For rationalism history becomes irrelevant and the contents of revelation consist only of abstract truths. But this rationalism was undermined by Kant and Schleiermacher. In his criticism of pure reason, Kant showed how we, if we had only been rational beings, would not know anything of God, the soul, liberty, or immortality indubitably. And he was very pleased with this result. He argued that religion, ethics, and theology would be better served if separated from rational proofs. He had been, after all, a witness to how rationalist theology failed to maintain itself over against empiricism. Kant saw how the demand of conscience required a more solid foundation for morals, theology, and religion. He was willing to sacrifice reason because, in addition to independent reason, he maintained an untouchable place for faith. Morality, conceived of in combination with the idea of God, thus became the foundation and content of religion.

From radically different premises, Schleiermacher came to a similar result, since he also regarded the Absolute and non-contradictable as unknowable to the human mind, which always operates within the framework of contrasts and contradictions. But while Kant regarded the revelation of God as a categorical imperative demanded by the commandments of the moral law, Schleiermacher claimed that the Absolute can only be experienced through feeling. With Kant, religion consists primarily of moral action, with Schleiermacher in sentiment. This ethical and mystic conception played a major role in nineteenth-century theology. And it is currently the case that the latter view is increasingly driving away the former. Even the neo-Kantianism of Ritschl's time has already been widely discarded. Younger scholars criticize Ritschl for one-sidedly interpreting religion exclusively in the ethical sense, without regard for the mystical. Ritschl fails to account for the contributions of Schleiermacher, and this mistake needs to be corrected. Religion is nothing other than personal piety, an experience of the soul, a sentiment, and a relationship with God which can only be experienced by both God and the individual as the parties in that relationship. For them, it above all boils down to that which is personal and mysterious. The enthusiasts and the apocalypticists are the true religious devotees. This point is even made by selecting certain events from history and representing them in plays. Not only theologians, but also literary scholars, historians, and artists preoccupy themselves with this. Just like art must be studied through the works of the masters, so the essence of religion is known primarily by means of its prophets and seers. Its content is not of primary concern, but only its strength and personal power. In this view, it is not only religion that is entirely swallowed up in sentiments and feelings, but also nature and history, art and science, and even theology that are sacrificed at the altar of secularization.

Religion has nothing to do with theology, which is itself reduced to a simple, historical science.

It must be admitted that this view is consistent and does not shy away from any of its implications. But it is based on a complete mischaracterization of the essence of religion. All religion, after all, has an inescapable truth claim and can only continue to exist for as long as its adherents are convinced of that truth. The emotion that religion effectuates in the hearts of people fades away as soon as its objective truth is discarded. The neo-romantic conception of religion does not take this into account and presents religion as something unrelated to truth and morality as well as something which spontaneously arises from the mood and feelings of man. Religion then becomes a matter of taste and private personal preference, which is of no more than aesthetic value to anyone but the individual believer himself. There is no revelation of God in nature, and history is considered to be foundational to religion itself. At most, there is in the deepest sentiments of man a kind of religious feeling and attraction to that which is eternal—one which finds unique expression in all the different religions and which the virtuous of all religions interpret and apply in their unique fashion. These interpretations, however, are wholly subjective and do not claim to be truthful per se. They only have value inasmuch as they provide a striking expression of the sentiments of the human heart. The ideal is therefore also the unification of religions, and Christians, Muslims, and Buddhists embrace one another as has been recently done in the Chicago City Council. There is little wonder that there is a strong resistance against such syncretism. Here in the Netherlands, there are even modernists who now advocate for a return to Christian theism, for the rightful place of metaphysics, for the immortality of the soul, and in part also for orthodox Christological doctrines. In Germany, there is an increasing chorus of voices who, against Haeckel and Ladenburg, also recognize the existence of a revelation of God in both nature and history, and consequently advocate for harmony between religion and science.[8]

He who takes religion seriously can in no way limit revelation to the mystical operation of human sentiment. Man is not isolated in the world but intrinsically bound to his surroundings and the context of his

---

[8] As Professor Van der Waals has noted in his essay on the phenomenon of the sea from 1903: "Everything in nature is the manifestation of the all-encompassing divine thought or will. Behind everything, there is an intelligent design because everything is bound to rules and laws." And so too Professor Bakhuis Roozeboom concludes in his Leiden lecture addressing the current problems in chemistry in 1904 as follows: "The further we delve into unchartered territory, the more reason there will be to stand in awe of the divine order, which also reveals itself in the field of nature and which leads back to the only true Source of all things."

existence. Just as a man who cannot satisfy his hunger with food starves to death, so the religious man is impoverished if he isolates himself from the world in an attempt to live off his sentiments alone. In the past, all those for whom religion truly was a matter of the heart differed from this position. Nature and history were regarded as the one revelation of God.[9] All of creation was seen as the manifestation of this revelation. If this position is true, then all the works of God need to be understood as revelation. And this is inevitable, because either all of creation is not a revelation of God, in which case it would not be His creation but would have to have some other origin, or it is the work of God both in terms of its origin and its perseverance, in which case it would have to reveal something about God.

If God reveals Himself in all His works, then it follows that not all elements of this revelation will always and everywhere be the same. The world is, after all, an organic whole that exhibits the greatest diversity in its unity. God's wisdom and omnipotence, His goodness and holiness are therefore revealed in different ways and to different degrees in His creations: in the organic more so than in the non-organic, and the reasonable more so than in the reasonless. In the history of man as an

---

[9] Bavinck's sentence will be confusing for some. The idea that he is explaining bears resemblance to Hegel's pantheistic idea that history *must* unfold the way it does, for it is essence, or nature, revealing itself *in* history.—Ed.

individual and of mankind as a whole, we
encounter antitheses, which cannot be in an
equal sense traced back to God. Regardless of
any attempts by monism to cast evil as a
necessary development in creation, for those
who are religiously and morally conscious,
truth and lies, holiness and sin, justice and
guilt always maintain their antithetical
character. Sin cannot occur apart from God's
governance but is not His work in the sense
that that which is good is. And this antithesis
also pertains to religion. It is simply a form of
pantheistic monism to regard all these as links
in a single chain or as moments in an ongoing
process, simply differing in degree and manner
in terms of revealing God. Precisely because
there is no religion without any
presuppositions, religions cannot be ranked,
but act as each other's antithesis. Those who
disregard this contrast and antagonism not
only disregard the nature of religion but also
relativize the distinction between truth and
falsehood and good and evil. They quietly
presume that there exists no law for the
religious and moral life and that religion is
nothing more than a sentiment that can differ
from person to person. In practice, of course,
no one holds to this theory. Anyone who finds
salvation in his religion would necessarily
oppose all others, and he does this all the more
as his faith strengthens. Even he who views
religion as merely a sentiment opposes all
those who do not share this view. It is also
foolish to regard the worship of nature,

Buddhism, Islam, Christianity, or even Roman Catholicism and Protestantism, as different stages of development of the same religion. If the pope is the infallible vicar of Christ, then the Reformation was the greatest folly. If the Mass had been instituted by Christ, then our communion is to be condemned.

Furthermore, it cannot be rightly claimed that religions only differ in terms of their presentation of truth while their deepest sentiments remain the same. Even deeper psychological analysis proves this false. There are a number of visible similarities between the various religions, of course. All religions, in belonging to one *genus*, have similar characteristics: they all have dogmatic, cultic, and ethical elements, and all have ideas of divinity and of sin and of redemption. But just as their presuppositions radically differ and stand in opposition to one another, so do their sentiments. It is, I admit, the same forces of the human soul which are activated through religiosity; but through differing presuppositions, they are guided towards differing directions, and therefore they have different persons and matters as objects. The love which binds a man to his wife is the same power of the soul which entices another man to commit adultery. But who would dare say that the disposition of the soul was the same in both cases and that they differ only in their practical outworking? This was taught by Romanticism and is today also taught by certain damnable movements in the arts. But no worthy man would ever even consider embracing such a moral anarchy. It directly contradicts the moral law. And it would be even worse to embrace with regard to religion the idea that only sentiments and disposition effectuate any differences. We must rather conclude that if God, by means of His moral law laid down the norms for human interaction, then it is most certainly true that He thereby laid down the norms for human interaction with Himself. The commands of the second table of God's law are built upon and founded upon the first table thereof.

There is also another way of showing how the various religions are not merely manifestations of the revelation of the same God. Christianity maintains a very distinct place among religions, in particular, because it condemns all others as false idolatry. All of Scripture bears witness to the fact of Christ as the Son, the Word, and the Image of God who has revealed God and His name to us. To this fact the experience of the Church also bears witness. Millions of believers have testified that through faith in this gospel, they have become inheritors of a communion with God that they had not known prior and received a new life that stands in direct contradistinction to their old sinful nature. They learned to boast with Paul in the peace of God and the blood of the cross. If this common experience of the faithful through the ages is no fantasy, but truthful, and the Christian religion, therefore, maintains a distinct place distinguished from all other religions, then this can only be clarified by means of the fact that the revelation which comes to us through Christ is very particular and unique. It is upon the distinct uniqueness of Christianity that special revelation rests, and therein it finds its origin.

I regard it as redundant to discuss here whether or not this special revelation is supernatural. In a certain sense, all true revelation is supernatural in terms of its origin and content. All revelation, properly understood, presupposes a world behind and above the natural world, which enters this world and reveals itself by both common and uncommon means. All revelation presupposes that God is, as a Personal Being, distinct from the world, but reveals Himself in and through the world. Naturalism and revelation are mutually exclusive. The uniqueness of Christianity presupposes the uniqueness of the Revelation upon which it is built. This has also been at the heart of apologetic battles of the Christian Church. It has always pertained to the uniqueness, independence, and absolute character of Christianity. In the battle against Ebionism and Gnosticism, against Arianism and Sabellianism, against Pelagianism and Manicheanism—the dispute had always been whether Christianity is the only true religion or whether it is only one option among many. This question is principally answered by the position Christ occupies in that religion. What does it confess regarding Christ? This perpetually remains the central question.
Undoubtedly, the attitude of any individual towards Christ is not only determined by

rational considerations alone. However, it is also true that the Church of Christ can utilize solid rational proofs in defense of its faith. Every heresy which in the name of Scripture falsely polemicized against the Church's confession, or which in the name of Christ falsely polemicized against Scripture, ended with the admission that the Church is built upon the foundation of the apostles and the prophets. But the attitude of anyone towards Christ and consequently towards all of revelation is not itself the fruit of rational argumentation but of deeply held religious and ethical motives. According to Dr. Bruining, there are, even among the modernists, a large group of scholars who still reserve a place for Christology in their dogmatics and recognize the importance of Christ not only for the religious development of humanity but also for personal religious life.[10] Similar, but much deeper and richer, is the experience of the Church. Her religious and moral life is intrinsically bound to the Person of Christ. From whence would a person who stands guilty

---

[10] Even so, if the modernists still believe in the existence of sin, in the essential distinction between good and evil, in the power of goodness, in the moral purpose and destiny of man, in the immortality of the soul, in God as the Father in Heaven, then they still don't believe that on the basis of rational proofs or as a result of the consistent application of the empirical method, but by other means, essentially employing the religious-ethical method, as Pierson notes in his book *Gods wondermacht en ons geestelijke leven*, 65.

before God acquire the confidence to approach God, to call Him Father, and to place in Him all his trust in crisis and in death, if God had not first approached us through Christ and reconciled the world to Himself in Him, thereby not regarding our sins anymore? If Christ had only been a normal person, or even a religious hero, His message regarding the conviction of sin would be as fallible and untrustworthy as any word of man. And if He had proclaimed this without satisfying the wrath of God towards sin through His suffering and death, he would have done nothing but proclaim the heresy that God does not justly punish sin. Therefore, not the righteous who are depressed by their guilt, but the godless who live carelessly would thereby be vindicated by Christ. The forgiveness of sins thereby becomes a phrase based on an outdated conviction. And sin thereby becomes an act regarded as a punishable offense not by God but by man alone. But this is not what sin is. And those who concern themselves and acknowledge its impious character cannot simply instantly become children of God and claim His grace without something happening. The gospel of the forgiveness of sins can only truly take away our sense of guilt as long as it proclaims that the moral law may never be broken. Then alone we can believe that we are justified before God even if our conscience accuses us, since God has, by means of undeserved grace alone, counted us righteous for Christ's sake. Thus, there exists an unbreakable and inseparable bond between the forgiveness of sins and the person and work of Jesus Christ. A similar bond exists between the revelation of God through Scripture and all of the religious experiences of the Church and its members regarding being children of God and being in communion with Him, regarding regeneration and the new man, regarding faith and prayer, and regarding perseverance and the hope of glory. Revelation and religion completely correlate. The latter impoverishes to the same degree that the former is limited. He who denies the reality of revelation in nature and in history and limits it to an operation of God in human consciousness, not only removes the very foundation upon which religion rests but also makes a great concession to arbitrariness and bigotry. True religion proves its own truthfulness in that it is founded upon a revelation that is not only known to the whole world by means of the works of God's hands but which also in a most unique fashion proclaims God's gracious forgiveness in accordance with the divine demand for obedience to His moral commandments.

The Blessings Bestowed By Christianity Upon Science

True religion, both as idea and praxis, obviously includes faith in the existence and knowability of God through both general and special revelation as its own objective truth. The history of religion undoubtedly confirms this. He who reduces the essence of religion to mere vague sentiments and influences has not come to this conclusion by means of objective historical research but on the basis of a specific philosophical view. But even if representation is an essential element of every religion, it still is unique in that it is not, like scientific findings, the result of either observation through the senses or of rational argument, but is always, as undoubted conviction of faith, rooted in the heart and is essential to the most intimate parts of human existence. Every religion, even the most syncretistic ones, pertains to the highest and holiest elements of human existence. That which is regarded as the highest and truest element of life is also the content of religion.[11] This very brief confession

---

[11] In my work *The Certainty of Faith* (Kampen: 1903), 72, I write: "Harnack has even in recent times claimed that the Person of Christ does not properly belong in the message of the gospel. The *Kerkelijke Courant* commented on this and argued that I failed to understand his claim in the proper context and therefore failed to understand its true meaning. Indeed, the words of Harnack in his *Das Wesen des Christenthums* are as follows: 'Not the Son, but the Father alone which the Son had proclaimed, belongs in the gospel.' But the fact that Jesus proclaimed the Father changes nothing to the central message of the gospel. However, according to Harnack, all of the gospel pertains to the relationship between God and the human soul, and neither the tax collector in the temple, the widow with her few coins, nor the prodigal son knew anything about any kind of Christology. Jesus therefore would have no place as Redeemer in the gospel. Harnack does of course add that

Christ knew the Father in a very particular manner (although he fails to explain how Christ came to this particular knowledge) and that, by means of His words and even more so by His deeds, Christ drew people closer to God and to the knowledge of God. He also acknowledges that His life and death have incredible significance for the world. But this amounts to nothing more than counting Jesus among the great men of history. The *Kerkelijke Courant* makes the same claim: 'Of a Christology that is a unique understanding of the essence, origin, and significance of the Son as well as the need for faith in Him as prerequisite for faith in the Father, there is no mention in the Lord's Prayer, in the parables of the tax collector in the temple, the widow with her few coins, nor of the prodigal son, and yet all these characters were justified in accordance with how Jesus related these narratives. But if it is so, then the words of Jesus are still the source and life of the gospel, and His Person and work its contents.

Therefore, when it comes to the question of whether Jesus belongs in the gospel, and whether there ought to be a *locus de Christo* in dogmatic theology, Dr. Bruining wisely notes: 'For Christ, the founder of Christianity, there is no place in dogmatics, which does not set out to treat history. Christ, the Founder and Leader of our religious life, must be acknowledged under the locus regarding the revelation of God as the First Means of that revelation. Christ, as the God-man and as the Mediator between God and the world, by Whom God has implanted the knowledge necessary for salvation, should form a separate locus in dogmatics on His own.' (*Teylers Theologische Tijdschrift* I, 449). Harnack's doctrine is reminiscent of Schleiermacher's claim that there has never been a school of religion developed which advocated an idea to be embraced for its own sake, but also for the sake of the one embracing it, and that many would tolerate that the means advocated could be therefore also entails an entire worldview, to which science is necessarily bound. This is because this confession entails the conviction of the existence of God, His unity, His Personality, His Fatherhood, His creation, His providence and governance of that creation, the unity of mankind, the particularity of the human relationship towards God, God's direction of history (in particular in the establishment of His Church), the redemption of mankind through the Person of Jesus, and the eventual glory of the Kingdom of God. All materialist, pantheist, and deist science are therefore presuppositionally excluded as false. The idea of "presuppositionless science" is itself utterly false. This short confession necessarily places us upon a theistic foundation and entails that, when we address any important geological, anthropological, psychological, or historical questions, we would do so by means of studying Scripture and through faith in the Person of Christ, and therefore could never be so-called "neutral, objective researchers." Even among the modernists in the Netherlands, there are those who acknowledge that we cannot practice any kind of Christian science unless the foundational philosophical presuppositions of the Christian faith have been accepted. If we, as Professor Bruining claims, want to maintain

---

set aside if only the true spirit and principle of the religion were to be embraced."

the orthodox religion, then we would have to force philosophy to accept its system of doctrine. Then we as theologians would have to once again direct philosophy because by such a means alone we would be able to ensure a place for religious faith in the realm of science.[12] Such an admission from the liberal school has great significance. It, after all, implies that religion indeed has an impact on science and that theologians could take the lead in philosophy. If the same would be claimed from the side of the orthodox, it would probably be condemned as heretical fanaticism. But the claim itself as it stands from Professor Bruining principally entails that which is confessed by every religious person who believes in the existence of truth. Religious faith necessarily demands that science takes it into account. Which religious faith is the right and truthful one also cannot be decided by any earthly judge. That must be made out by each individual personally in his conscience before God. If the Roman Catholic submits to the authority of the pope, the Reformed Christian to that of Holy Scripture, and the modernist arranges his life in accordance with his own conscience, then it in each case rests upon a personal choice. This of course does not imply

---

[12] See Dr. Bruining's "Religion and Liberty" in *Addresses and Papers at the Second Internal Council of Unitarian and other liberal religious thinkers and workers held in Amsterdam* (September 1903. Edited by P.H. Hugenholtz, Leiden: Brill), 177-178.

that it is immaterial which choice is made as long as it is made genuinely since subjective sincerity is no measurement for objective truth. But as people, we have no right to force others in matters of religion since each is his own master in this regard. Heresy and truth, weeds and wheat will always continue to co-exist here on earth and continue to grow alongside each other until the day of the harvest. And He who can make an infallible separation between good and evil is God alone. This truth was also proclaimed against the Roman Catholic Church by the Reformers by means of their doctrine of *facultas Sacra Scripturae se ipsam interpretandi*. Not by violence and suppression, not by political force or by law, but by means of the royal way of liberty, truth must achieve its victory.

For this reason, Christian scientific scholarship also has a full right to existence. If religion can impact the realm of science, and if every religious confession necessarily impacts scientific investigations and scientific interpretations, then age-old Christian convictions may not be reduced to unscientific dogmatism. Among many now there exists the conviction that Christianity is opposed to all culture and in particular science and the arts. But such a view is equally false as the formerly widely held idea that Christianity is nothing more than the gospel of humanity. These views are just as subject to the fashions of the day as are clothing and decorations. Ever since the apostolic witness was made subject to independent judgment, people have tried to invent their own Jesus. Kant saw in Him a manifestation of the divine sonship of mankind; Renan embraced Him as an opponent to the rule of the clergy; Proudhon regarded Him as a social reformer; Schopenhauer elevated Him to a symbol of the "negation" of life, while others have cast Him as a theosophist, an ascetic, or viewed Him as the pure archetype of the Aryan or Germanic race. In reality, these people only embrace from the revelation of Christ in the New Testament that which is most suitable to their own philosophy, thereby reconstructing the ideal Christ in accordance with modernist tastes. But any such theology, even if deemed scientific, cannot claim to be true.

Jesus did not act as a Reformer of state and society, nor did he dedicate His life to practicing the arts or the sciences. What He brought us was something radically different and infinitely higher. In His Person, His words, and His work, He brought us the gospel of God's grace: He brought the Kingdom of God to earth and through His righteousness opened the gates thereof to us. The gospel is the message of salvation for guilty and lost sinners. This it has always been, and this it must remain. But precisely because of this, it is an immense blessing to all of humanity and the world, to the state and society, to the arts, and to science.

The first thing for which science is indebted to the gospel is the reality of an eternal and unchanging truth. The concept of science did not originate from Christianity. All of history is marked by the human search for truth. Science originated in Greece, and the concept was invented by the ancient Greek philosophers. But despite all of its breakthroughs and sharp research, it could not maintain the heights it had reached in the days of Socrates, Plato, and Aristotle, as it was soon made subject to practical ends and was eventually completely destructed along with the entire ancient culture. It was unable to provide a unity to knowledge nor to satisfy the needs of the human heart, as the world with all its wisdom did not know God.

It was Christianity that saved science. The gospel proclaimed an eternal, undoubted, absolute truth, revealed in Christ, thereby rescuing science from the skepticism into which it had declined. Even Du Bois-Reymond admits that it "was through the monotheistic religions of the Jews, Christians, and Muslims that the concept of an absolute truth entered the world." The idea that there exists an absolute and unchanging truth knowable to mankind is foundational to all science. Christianity introduced this idea. And this truth is no subjective representation or an interrelationship of various human representations, but an objective reality—far above, yet still acquirable by man. Thereby science has been provided with a set, coherent, and unmissable foundation. For if in matters of religion and morality, or in spiritual or metaphysical matters, there can be no certainty acquired, science loses a great deal of its value and becomes vulnerable to skepticism and eventually complete destruction.

It is true that now science has been elevated to almost immeasurable heights, but it is still partially based upon Christian foundations. Inasmuch as science, therefore, seeks to overthrow these foundations, it contributes to its own destruction. The proofs of these are already evident. As on the one hand as skepticism, fatigue, and doubt increase, men are driven into the hands of the most preposterous superstition. There also exists no guarantee that the culture in which we pride ourselves will not one day be taken away from us. Those of Babylon and Assyria, Greece and Rome declined despite all of the heights they had achieved. Who can predict the future of our civilization? Who does not tremble at the thought of the red, black, or yellow danger?[13]

---

[13] Bavinck's statement can be interpreted, and meant, either ontologically or epistemologically. For example, suppose a hypothetical war takes place between Africa and Europe. Such a statement, if interpreted ontologically, would be saying that Europe is at war with Africa *because* of skin color. The more charitable interpretation is epistemological; by which an enemy is made known, not a statement of cause. Thus, such and such a character trait characterizes one's enemy. In short, this would parallel the modern question of whether or not a police officer is racist for describing the suspect by skin color. As a helpful identifier, such descriptions should not be considered racist.—Ed.

As Fickler notes:

> No, the belief in an unmitigated development of humanity (as thought of by Hegel) is untenable. As Willamowitz-Moellendorf has noted in his imperial speech, the idea of the periodical rise and fall of civilizations is no mere speculation, as world history has proven itself to not be marked by linear progress. It is important to remember that what appears to be inalienable gain by human labor can also be lost. Cultures can die as they have in the past. The jackals now howl in Ephesus where Heraclitus and Paul once preached. Thorns and bushes now cover the marble halls of hundreds of formerly great cities in Asia Minor. Desert sands swirl over the formerly great gardens of Kyrenia. But why use only pictures from afar? Anyone who simply remembers the great Roman Forum must conclude that eternal and continuous progress is delusional. The resistance of evil is far too great and effective to reduce all of history to a scheme of thesis, antithesis, and synthesis.

By preaching an objective truth, Christianity has planted a belief in and a love of truth in the hearts of men. Just as the existence of an objective truth is the foundation of science, so the love of truth is the unmissable subjective condition for it. But a love of truth is not characteristic of natural man. There is no virtue in depravity. In practice, we often witness how truth is sacrificed for self-interest. And those who practice science are no exception to this rule. They are no better or worse than others who work in trade or industry, in the state, or in society. Once there is a coincidental overlap between truth and self-interest, there is no difficulty in being a friend of truth. But it often happens in the field of science that truth is at odds with our wishes, desires, or dispositions. How often is there not a contradiction between mind and heart, between reason and will or desire, or between tendencies and duty? Then sharp self-evaluation and self-criticism are needed in order to remain true to the truth and not to falsify it in service of the desires of the heart. There are many truths people live in denial of because they are at odds with their desires. Here the words of Christ, namely that those who love their lives will lose them, are most relevant. And this enables us to understand the gospel, for it teaches us a truth that we could never acquire other than by denying ourselves. The gospel of Christ provides science with an ethical character and sanctifies its practice. Bacon rightly regards the realm of science to be one which, just like the Kingdom of Heaven, cannot be entered unless we become like children.

The science known as theology is, for its very existence, indebted to Christianity. Many nowadays have no high regard for this field, however. From various sides, it is being attacked and its scientific character is underappreciated. And theologians themselves have helped effectuate this by not taking up the cause of defending theology as a science, but so often making needless concessions out of fear whenever some or another scholar expresses any kind of criticism, thereby surrendering bulwark after bulwark. She who had previously been known as the queen of the sciences has reduced herself to being a beggar among her sisters. She would be willing to surrender theology altogether as long as she is only allowed to remain religious studies. Nonetheless, theology remains a most noble science which exists only thanks to Christianity. Even in pagan religions, there exists an element of truth, however. God is not unknown to anyone, and through His creation He makes His eternal power and divinity known. But this knowledge of truth is mixed with so many heresies and lies that there can be no mention of theology as a science among the pagans. As soon as scientific thought arose in ancient Greece, it occupied a position not within, but in opposition to the religious beliefs of the people. The history of the Christian Church testifies, however, to the rise of a theological scholarship as a science born from the very faith of the Church, and which is directed towards the knowledge of God and the increasing cultivation thereof. As long as she remains true to this and perseveres in what she was always supposed to be, she will retain her position as the queen of the sciences. Her preeminent position is itself not guaranteed by the men who practice theology, even if the Church has produced, from the days of the apostles, an undeniable host of eminent and most notable scholars,[14] who tower in comparison to those of our age; but her eminence is the result of her object of study. Theology pertains to the most elevated objects and the most intimate convictions of human life. It treats those questions which are of the highest importance to every human being without distinction. Without denying the importance of mathematics, natural science, philology, or history, they simply do not bear the same weight as the truths of theology.[15] It is thus not the desire for dominance on the part of theologians, but the central place and the significance of religion and morality for all of

---

[14] It has long been a common practice to speak of an *odium theologicum*, because theologians often occupy themselves with matters pertaining to the very heart of human life, which are therefore also of great interest to non-theologians, but this is also true of the arts, trade, commerce, etc. We read, for example, how Haeckel treats his opponents. See E. Dennert's *Die Wahrheit über Ernst Haeckel und seine Welträdsel* (Halle, 1903), 62.

[15] As Thomas Aquinas notes in his *Summa Theologica I* question 1, article 5, reply 1: "The most insignificant of knowledge which can be obtained from the highest things is still more desirable than the most certain knowledge acquired from the lesser things."

human life which ensures theology the title of Queen of the Sciences. Even Professor Bruining, at a recent conference of liberal religious thinkers, emphasized the need for theologians to once again act as trendsetters in the field of philosophy. Theology would only be able to satisfy this demand if it proclaims a truth that rests upon divine authority and which stimulates the human conscience. But if we reject God's Word, what wisdom is there left for us?

In the third place, Christianity is also a blessing for science in general, and in particular for scholarship on nature and history. Ladenburg oversimplifies the matter in his famous speech at a conference for scientists and doctors at Cassel, wherein he ascribes the scientific progress of recent times to the "Enlightenment" alone. If he is confronted with the fact that naturalists have completely destroyed the happiness of mankind, undermined the faith in immortality, and replaced this with only factories and social misery, then he argues that the new understanding of liberty and human rights, the abolition of slavery and social legislation, is all thanks to the "Enlightenment," which was principally brought about by science. Even if natural science has delivered very significant results for modern society and has borne much fruit, it is most inappropriate to attribute all the benefits of modern society to science. Society is not so simply constituted. Many different factors contribute thereunto.

However, if we speak of the blessing bestowed upon science by Christianity, we do not mean to imply that science is solely the product of Christianity. Science does not arise from redemption but from creation. And the Christian religion does not in the first place aim at producing culture. Earthly prosperity, high civilization, and scientific development are not the standards of its truth and value. What the Christian religion principally offers us is the comfort to live and to die saved. But in doing so, it sanctifies all of man, his entire life and being, and all of his thought and action. And therefore, Christianity also fruitfully sanctifies science.

Christianity is the only force capable of preserving mankind from declining into materialism and pantheism, or into scientific and ethical skepticism. For many scholars there now exists only one science, namely natural science. Literature, history, law, religion, ethics—all of the ideals of mankind are regarded as inferior, and the sciences which occupy themselves with these are only worthy of the name insofar as they adopt the method of natural science. The cynical indifference and gross ignorance of many of these men when it comes to these spiritual goods of mankind has been evidenced by representatives from all the schools which have developed from Haeckel's work on the mysteries of the world. And Ladenburg in his much-discussed speech has provided us with further proof of this when he notes that, "The sacredness of the Bible could only be rightly appreciated once it was recognized as a work of man just like all others." Even if with the ancient Greeks the origins of science had been most noble, during the Middle Ages a deep darkness spread over man: "Ignorance and superstition became the governing powers during the Middle Ages, which was followed by intolerance, inquisition, the persecution of witches, and religious insanity." But men like Columbus, Copernicus, Kepler, and Newton brought light in the darkness; science was awakened, and humanity made tremendous strides forward. But now it is recognized as having only been a dream: "a presumptuous and completely unfounded dream, which stimulated man's close relationship with his Creator, who supposedly created him in His image." That there is no real supernatural revelation in the Bible is evident to Ladenburg, who notes that "the Old Testament is a work of fantasy and even the New Testament cannot be considered to be of divine origin." There were never any miracles: "All phenomena are natural, and notions of the supernatural arise only in the minds of lunatics and the ignorant." God cannot be anything more than an "embodiment" of natural laws. Immortality is nothing more than a desire on the part of man.

Thus, in a short address of merely a couple of pages, the entire traditional worldview is swept aside. If this lecture amounted merely to an isolated instance, one could easily just ignore it. However, it was precisely because Haeckel's *Weltradsel* had sold thousands upon thousands of copies that Professor Ladenburg delivered his short address to a notable gathering of German scientists and doctors. For this, he received only the greatest of praise, including in the press. When viewed in light of other recent scientific developments, as well as those in the literature and the arts, it then becomes evident that the materialism of a Büchner, even in spite of the recent revival of idealism, is still very much alive and well in the minds of the common people. It is, after all, not a particular verse in Scripture, but the entire Christian worldview, which Ladenburg seeks to dismantle—the very belief in a personal God and the immortality of the soul, even if he stops short from going as far as Strauss and expresses himself in a more nuanced fashion. Therefore, it ought to awaken a great interest among the general population when Christians warn about the threat posed by materialism, not only for religion or Christianity, but also for morality, law, truth, science, and the arts. We now find much sympathy for our position in terms of our desire to rebuild culture and science upon Christian foundations, thereby ensuring their continued existence. For our part, we can also appreciate the criticism leveled against theoretical and practical materialism by idealism. But if this idealism is not built upon the Christian faith, it almost always either dissolves into pantheism or self-destructs. Only the Christian religion, by acknowledging the independence of the human spirit and recognizing our unique position in contradistinction to the world around us can protect idealism against both these tragedies. It is Christianity which reveals the realm of invisible and eternal things to us, brings us into contact with these, and allows us to be strengthened by them over against being ruled by nature, and which gives meaning to our person, our calling, and our work. The history of science bears witness to the fact that this religious idealism has proven to be most beneficial to it. In part, this had even been true for men such as Socrates, Plato, and Aristotle who, to the shame of many Christians, made most excellent use of the light which they were granted. But it is particularly true for all the men of science over the centuries who have in fact been driven by their Christianity to further scientific knowledge. In many circles, there is currently a prevalent notion that the great scientists of the past had not been Christians, but the exact opposite is true. And had historians of the various sciences—historians of philosophy in particular—not systematically and deliberately concealed the religious convictions of scholars' past, this fact would be much more widely known.

It furthermore needs to be emphasized that the best modern approaches to science or history either implicitly or explicitly presuppose the principles of Christianity. Their conceptions of nature and history are fundamentally rooted in Christianity. And the inevitable consequence of researchers turning their backs upon Christianity is that their research greatly suffers. Materialist science, for example, has for many years emphasized the coincidental and purposeless mechanism of nature in order to liberate nature from morality. In a certain sense, it rightly resisted the idolatry of nature which had been associated with idealism. But in the process, it has also descended into the alternative extreme. It has completely separated nature from its divine origin. Consequently, this same nature, which is ironically now better understood than ever before, has become to so many a mystical and almost demonic force, as it is so often portrayed in literature and art. Thereby, superstition once again reemerges. God has disappeared from natural scholarship and the devil has taken His place. With Nietzsche, there is no coherent concept of nature. The entire world consists of chaos without order, law, or design. He poses the question of when nature will be completely de-divinized and answers that this will only be accomplished when all laws, order, standards, and logic have been separated from natural phenomena.

The same dynamic manifests itself in historiography when this is separated from the Christian religion. If there is no personal God who governs all things by means of His providence, what ground then remains to believe that there is purpose to history? Schopenhauer realized this, and consequently denied the existence of any historical progress. For him, history is merely the endless and purposeless repetition of distress and calamity—the result of blind forces. While Hegel acknowledged the existence of a certain reason behind reality, Schopenhauer identified it with chaos. And indeed, if historical materialism entails that thought is not the origin of being, but being the origin of thought, then the central scientific presupposition that there is a logic and plan underlying reality is completely discarded. This presupposition can only be maintained through Christian theism which acknowledges that nature itself is the work of God and that history is the manifestation of the providential guidance of His omnipotent hand.

When this major and decisive agreement between Christianity and true science is considered, all other perceived or apparent differences become trivial. In itself, it may seem of great significance, since it pertains to the origin of the world and humanity, the revelation of God through Israel and in the Person of Jesus Christ. But in principle, all these disputes are decided by Christian theism, for it concentrates upon the supernatural. If the question regarding the supernatural could be reduced to Professor Ladenburg's oversimplification that "all which presents itself in nature is natural and all that is supernatural proceeds from the mind and imagination of the ignorant," then I suppose it would have been a waste of time and paper to address this issue any further. But the supernatural world is inseparable from the theistic confession and is of tremendous religious and ethical significance. The supernatural proves that the mechanism of the world is subservient to theology, that the physical realm is subservient to the ethical realm, and that the world is subservient to the Kingdom of God. If there is nothing supernatural and God is merely a human name and concept for natural laws, and if there is no higher power and design behind nature, then the spirit of man is made subservient to matter, all religious and ethical life loses its foundation, and the belief in the triumph of good over evil is but a vain dream. Arthur Titius therefore rightly called the belief in the supernatural the highlight of faith in divine providence. It is in no way at odds with the natural order, which in fact both presupposes and confirms it. There can also be no conflict between the supernatural and the scientific or historical method since it leaves this intact as it is always elevated above scientific scrutiny. Just as physiological psychology can trace how the titillation of our senses stimulates our mind, but remains in awe of the mystery of observation, so historical and natural sciences often approach the supernatural realm but can never pierce it. There is a mysterious force at work that it acknowledges by faith, but that it can never explain.

For this reason, an alliance between the Christian faith and science is not only possible but necessary. True religion and true science can simply never be at odds with each other. A strict separation between the two has been regarded by some as a necessary means for preserving the integrity of religion, but in the long run, it can only prove fatal. Both practically and theoretically, such a separation is untenable. How could it ever be upheld that a man, because of his fear of God, would be unsuitable for practicing science? To the contrary, godliness is beneficial for all things, including science. While it must be conceded that even the godly have their shortcomings and biases, this changes nothing regarding the principle. Love of God can never be at odds with love of one's neighbor or love of science, but is much rather the foundation, central principle, and driving force thereof. The goal of the scientific researcher is not to, in conducting his work, suppress the deepest and most noble convictions of his heart, but to be fully equipped, as a child of God, for all good works. Being a human being and being a Christian can never be at odds. The best Christians always make the best human beings.

4

The Christian University

The Christian scientific principles discussed
in this work have to be manifested in the
Christian university. The concept of a Christian
university itself is nothing new. All elementary
and high schools as well as universities in the
Netherlands had a distinctly Christian, even
confessional character until the beginning of
the nineteenth century. What is new is the
system described by Dr. Kuyper as the
"indifferent system," based on the so-called
neutral conception of the sciences. Whereas the
old system had proven its virtues, however, this
new conception of science still needs to prove
not only its tenability but its very possibility.

What it has shown us so far does not
bode well for its claim of neutrality. Its
neutrality merely consists of accommodating
all negative schools but transforms into
partiality whenever a positive Christian faith is
encountered. The shameless persecution of the

Reformed Separatists who split from the national Church in 1834 proves this. When Isaäc da Costa dared proclaim his objections against the spirit of the age, he was treated in Amsterdam as if he had been infected by leprosy. When Jan Jacob Van Oosterzee even mildly criticized the modernist doctrines prevalent in the Dutch Reformed Church—a criticism all now accept to have been just—his name was slandered within the scientific community at the University of Leiden. And these are not isolated instances, as the same had happened in the lives of Chantepie de la Saussaye and Nicolaas Beets, as well as that of Guillaume Groen van Prinsterer and now Abraham Kuyper. Nonetheless, in recent years there has been somewhat of a positive change and the glory days of liberalism seem to have passed, its arrogance snapped, and the proposal for confessional professors' chairs has been well-received, and the claim that there is no science possible on the basis of divine revelation has been largely subdued. But the significance of this change has also been overestimated by the likes of Professor van der Vlugt, who has gone as far as to say that there is no longer a need for a Christian university in the Netherlands. The recent changes have, after all, not been the result of liberal principles, but a consequence of the Christian opposition against them. It is therefore of a coincidental, rather than a principal nature, and came to be due to changing circumstances rather than from conviction. Toelstra, the leader of the

Social Democrats, has openly proclaimed his conviction that dogma and science are irreconcilable, and that their party is most pleased with the current condition of the universities, and therefore desire no change in this regard. The battle regarding the nature of science and the university is far from over, however. The battle pertains to matters which cannot be solved by means of a few benevolent comments. It pertains, such as Prime Minister Kuyper has noted in his parliamentary speeches, to the battle between the Christian and the non-Christian, or the old and the new worldviews, between creation and revelation on the one hand and evolution on the other. It pertains to the matters of sin and redemption, and fundamentally revolves around the question: What do you believe regarding Christ? This is why, whenever such matters of principle are discussed, the political parties are again divided to the right and to the left, not because of the preference of individual party members, but in accordance with the logic of principles. When it comes to this so-called "neutral science," it seems as though it is always acceptable to proceed from the philosophical principles of Spinoza, Kant, Hegel, Marx, Comte, Scholten, or Opzoomer, but never the principles of the confession of Christ according to the Scriptures.

But apart from this, the neutral conception and practice of science are also at odds with the reality of life. Universities aren't abstractions, but institutions with a particular history, bound by tradition, and which are influenced by their surroundings. However, as they have gradually developed into organs of the state, they have conceded their liberty and independence. Kant, therefore, even argued that science at the level of the university can only truly be practiced within the faculty of philosophy, as this faculty alone could be free, unprejudiced, and independent since it was exclusively bound to reason and could therefore serve truth. But the other faculties, he claimed—those of theology, law, medicine— were either bound to the laws of the state or by the practical limitations of human life. While he was a proponent of free inquiry in theory, he believed that science ought to be conducted in service of the highest ideal of mankind, the ethical community. Consequently, he often advocated great caution in practice. Although one should always make sure that one's claims are truthful, one should not proclaim all truth openly. The faith of the common people should also be approached with caution. The Bible and other accepted religious standards must therefore be utilized as means to cultivate a moral consciousness in the schools and the churches, where questioning the Bible would be unwise—otherwise, men only cultivate complete unbelief among the people. But men must rather, out of a love for the people, use the old ecclesiastical faith as a means of creating fertile soil for the new rational faith. Therefore, one must speak carefully, so as to avoid the risk of alienation and to protect oneself against the embarrassment of having to recant later. Kant acted accordingly. When he, in 1793, wrote his *Religion within the Bounds of Pure Reason*, and in reaction thereunto received an unappreciative letter from King Friedrich Wilhelm, he proclaimed that he, as a servant of the king, would refrain from any further discussion of natural or revealed religion.

The system of absolute freedom of investigation has, in principle, never been defended by anyone, nor has it ever been implemented in practice. Freedom of investigation needs to be carefully distinguished from freedom of conscience, religion, or the press. In a narrower sense, this entails that teachers at educational institutions ought to be able to openly proclaim their convictions. But this right is everywhere limited as it inescapably always is. The interests of the state, the maintenance of public order, old traditions, and good morals—all place limitations upon this freedom. If, for example, a public school teacher were to promote nihilism, anarchism, and the right to revolution and regicide, suicide, perjury, or polygamy, then it goes without saying that the state would not sit idly by and watch. Of course, there is a difference between advocating with one's words and committing with one's actions. But if the students were to be incited to action by the words of the teacher, there certainly would be reason for concern on the part of the state.

Yet all would acknowledge the difficulty with which the state would be faced when acting against such a teacher. In the first place, the modern state is supposedly neutral, and it has no confession and no standard of morality, thereby only being bound to a vague adherence to good morals and public order. But in many cases, it is in science, as it is in life, highly difficult to maintain a healthy balance between authority and liberty, or between conservation and progress. Next to authority, liberty also has its rights. Whenever something new is proclaimed, it is more often than not faced with resistance from various sides, even if it is later shown to be truthful. But precisely because the modern state lacks the competence and authority to guide over true principles, thereby allowing all kinds of teachings in its schools and universities, it ought to be most pleased with the fact that the people are erecting more and more Christian schools. Christian elementary schools erected in the past century have been widely acknowledged to have had a blessed impact upon the Dutch nation. The state, therefore, has no reason to regret adopting a friendlier stance towards them. And this is even more true for Christian middle and high schools. Now that the government has conceded its right to advance the Kingdom of Jesus Christ, it has become all the more important for it to, as a moral imperative, support and encourage all actions to this end undertaken by the nation itself.

The value of such endeavors is even further emphasized by the fact that one considers that universities are not only institutions of science, but also education and training. High schools and universities have two different tasks: cultivating science and training for practice. Even the most idealist school needs to take this double calling of the university into account. A school dedicated only to advancing science would have no students. Most of those who undertake a study do so in the first place to later acquire a position and start a career in the Church, the state, or in society. In this regard also life precedes philosophy—i.e., practice precedes theory. The popular motto of "practicing science for the sake of science" sounds nice, but it has no correlation to reality. All students seek, by means of the university, to establish a lifelong career. But even if training is therefore of the utmost importance, it is not the sole duty of the university, especially not those of the German type.

Undoubtedly, the practice of science is not limited to the university, just as it is not bound to a specific office, calling, or class. It develops freely from the human spirit itself, which has been endowed by God with the ability and disposition for scientific investigation. Many men who were never educated by or affiliated with a university, have, through the ages, practiced and cultivated science. All those who have, in either the fields of science or historiography, contributed to advancing science and fought ignorance by contributing to a better understanding of God's design belong to the *universitas scientarum*. But this changes nothing to the fact that the universities, by bringing together a large group of men of science and providing them with a career and resources, have developed into unique institutions of science. This practice of science is not at odds with the goal of training the youth for careers, even if it is not always easily harmonized with it. This is because the training for a career takes place at these very institutions by means of a distinctly scientific education, which cultivates independent thought and observation. It is precisely this scientific education that is the primary means by which the university cultivates clear insight and independent judgment.

It is often claimed that such a scientific training of independent-minded young men can only take place when students are taught by professors who hold a wide variety of contradictory positions. If this were the case, one would expect every university both in the Netherlands and abroad to have a wide variety of differing worldview-based professorships. In reality, however, this is not the case. On the contrary, universities and faculties are rather prone to employ staff of similar convictions, and the appointment of a professor from a dissenting worldview is the exception rather than the rule. The reason for this is obvious, as professors most commonly seek out the company of those with whom they have the most in common. For many years, in fact, Professor Van Geer was criticized for his appointments at public universities, since the faculties were consulted so as to exclude those from diverging opinions in an attempt to minimize conflict. This amplifies the disconnect between the liberal theory and practice. In theory, there is room for everyone, but in practice only for friends.

But the liberal position of neutrality is also psychologically and pedagogically untenable. It rests upon the presumption that the youth, having just completed high school, would be of their own accord able to independently make an informed decision between contrasting ideas, theories, principles, or systems. It is implicitly based on the idea that the mind as abstraction is the only standard by which human judgments are made, and that authority and faith, heart and conscience have no bearing upon our academic formation. At our high schools and universities, this reality is not taken into account nearly enough, and it is almost as if scholars are ashamed of it. Professors very rarely if ever address religious and moral issues, and on the rare occasions when they do so, they are treated as rational abstractions rather than realities of life. Even in the primary schools, we often hear the opinion expressed that teachers ought to be wholly unconcerned with the behavior of children outside of the classroom. School and life are thereby completely separated. And even at universities, education is now expected to be the responsibility of students themselves. It is little wonder that there are now warnings issued against such a system of education—or rather lack of education—from within the universities themselves. How could a system of pedagogy wherein young men who have not even reached the age of twenty, without much practical experience regarding the hard realities of life, and who view everything with a radical one-sidedness, are told that they are to discard all authority and tradition in forming their own independent worldview? The consequence of such a system can be none other than that which has been aptly described by Professor Woltjer last year in parliament as a group of students who are inherently antagonistic towards education by a professor, and who reject from prejudice everything he teaches out-of-hand. In such a system, education is practically impossible. Even if a second group were to accept the authority of the professor, a third group would become entirely skeptical and be robbed of all hope, pragmatically directing themselves towards practice alone without any regard to principles.

Undoubtedly, a true university education includes impartially exposing students to alternative systems and views. This can, however, be done just as fruitfully in Christian institutions as in those with a so-called neutral character. Even if all the public schools and universities are neutral in the sense that no student or professor is excluded on the basis of his religious convictions, this does not imply that the students or professors themselves are neutral, since they all have distinct worldviews which they love and defend, and which serve as the framework for their research. In fact, it can rightly be claimed that it is at the Christian universities where alternative and opposing worldviews are more thoroughly studied since the public institutions have come to wholly embrace a modernist worldview which they consider to be fully in touch and in accordance with the spirit of the age. This is precisely because Christian universities self-consciously position themselves according to their convictions such that they exhibit an increased awareness of alternative philosophies of science. The scientific works of the faithful bear ample witness to this fact.

It is only natural that any faithful exposition of an alternative worldview by a Christian professor would be followed by a criticism based upon the conviction of the truth of the Christian worldview, but this is no less true of any professor at a so-called neutral university. If he is unsatisfied with the idea of not teaching but merely narrating, he would through his account of other positions necessarily use his own convictions as the standard in judging the opinions of others. Any principled man is also a propagandist. Even the skeptic propagandizes doubt. But this method most appropriately employed by professors does not in any way preclude the student's right and duty to critical evaluation through independent scientific investigation.

156 | The Christian Philosophy of Science

In practice also, no one actually works within a neutral framework. Just as the universities and faculties generally employ like-minded individuals, so parents as a rule send their children to institutions that are most agreeable to their own principles and convictions. The difference only consists therein that the modernists, liberals, radicals, and socialists are content with the current status quo, and consequently receive via the state the kind of schools they desire for their children, while Christians, not being content with the worldview taught at these schools, are forced to establish their own. Undoubtedly, the aforementioned parties would, if public schools in the Netherlands were either Reformed or Roman Catholic, do the very same, and complain about their rights to liberty and equality being violated.

The Christian university is furthermore preferable to the neutral university in that it acknowledges and restores the bond between theory and practice. The current condition of higher education is most unhealthy. It is most unbecoming that there currently exists such a chasm between school and life, between science and practice, or between theology and Church. In the field of religion, this is most apparent, but it is not only pastors who preach the heresies they have been taught at public universities to the faithful, but even lawyers, doctors, and teachers are generally now, in terms of their religious and moral convictions, at odds with the people they are supposed to serve. This cannot be considered normal. If these divisions cannot be reconciled, then this dualism threatens the very fabric of our civilization—which could, just like that of the ancients, collapse along with our religion. In reality, everyone is convinced of this fact. There is no esoteric or exoteric science, and there is no duality to truth.

There are those who claim that this dilemma or contradiction can only be solved if the people radically revise their religious and moral convictions in light of modern science. This demand is also often made to the Church by theologians themselves, but it is based upon the same idea. The proponents of the modernist worldview, evolutionists, moralists, and criminologists advocate this, and by means of the government, demand that Christian nations be liberated from their traditions, and their children already be introduced to the claims of modern science in elementary schools. This is why there is such a vigorous battle raging with regard to the schools. It pertains to the very question of whether the Christian or the modernist worldview will inform our national life in the future. Rightly therefore, Dr. Eduard David, the competent spokesman for the evolutionist Social Democrats, argues that the acquisition of political power through revolution has not yet been completed. He argues that it is,

...[not] the government officials, nor the leading spirits within the opposition parties who currently deny us political power, but rather the majority of the people behind these officials who oppose us, refuse to entrust us with power, and deny us the ability to enforce our policies. The idea is nothing new. But it appears that the profound speculation of our radicals are no simple insights. Therefore, it must once again be emphasized that the protection of backward reactionaries is the majority of the people, and the people are still their own worst enemy. The ignorance of the masses is the most serious obstacle in our path to gaining political power, and once this bulwark has been overcome, will there still remain any resistance to our spell?

Such words do not fall on deaf ears. But we surely hope that this bulwark, erected by the Christian confession of nations, would be able to fend off such a formidable attack. The attackers also do not realize what will have been destroyed once this bulwark is done away with, since he who takes from the nation its faith surrenders it to complete unbelief, and effectively pushes it into the arms of the worst kind of superstition. Kant already feared this consequence, and for this same reason, Hegel desired to preserve for the people only the mere form of the contents of the philosopher's convictions. Yet, if the religion of Christian nations is merely the same as the idolatries of pagan nations, then we ought to be opposed just like the Greek philosophers since heresy and lies can never bring about more than false liberty and false comfort.

Before discarding all hope of reconciliation, however, we ought to seriously consider the question of whether modern science, in terms of its principal method, as well as its results, is not fundamentally erroneous. And the question becomes even more salient once we consider what has already been advocated under the banner of modern science. Who can seriously desire its theories regarding the existence of God, Christ, the apostles, and prophets, the soul and its immortality, the origin of man and society, law and ethics, sin and crime, retribution and punishment, marriage and the family, or property and homicide to become the standard for our national consciousness and directive for our lives? Not only religion and morality, but the family, society, and the state would thereby be completely dismantled. The currently prevalent notion of science is at odds not only with the confession of the Church but with the very existence and life of humanity. It does not investigate reality; it distorts it. It does not explain life; it destroys it. If politicians recognize no higher authority than the will of the people, if sociologists identify a subconscious drive and arbitrary human will as the sole causes behind the initiation and development of society, if lawyers recognize no eternal norms which sanction law but only ever-changing human relationships and arrangements as its foundation, if criminologists regard each criminal as a victim of his own insanity and prison as a kind of educational institute, if moralists disregard all distinction between good and evil and glorify sexual licentiousness and suicide, if historians identify history solely as the operation of economic factors alone, if psychologists deny the independence of the human soul, if doctors regard their own practice and veterinary science to differ only in degree but not in nature, and if theologians no longer accept religious truth, then it is self-evident that the very foundation of civilization has been done away with. As such, the demand that modern science drastically revises its philosophy before reforming our society is a most holy and noble one.

Such a demand is also in fact made by the idealist school, which has been recently revived. But there are also those who have forsaken all hope of a revival of Christianity, a societal return to the gospel of Christ, or a principled restoration of science and society. But a university founded upon the foundation of the gospel and in accordance with the confession of the Church is by no means opposed to science, only to many of its contemporary practitioners. The gospel should be foundational to science as it by no means inhibits its development, but rather protects those who practice it—limited, sinful people with a depraved mind and an insidious heart—

from heresy and error and enables them to better search for truth. Science, after all, entails the search for truth. However, if some of its contemporary spokesmen are to be believed, you would think that liberty as opposed to truth has always been its end. Liberty, however, is but a means to the end of truth. Liberty as an abstract concept is furthermore very difficult to define. Just as it is on the one hand threatened by enslaving chains, so it must guard against arbitrariness and relativism. Scientific freedom principally consists in the right to search for truth and to promote and defend truth wherever it is found. But while here on earth there exists no infallible organ to be employed by science, scientific freedom also entails that neither the state nor the Church suppress the rights of the different scientific schools to employ their respective methods in the search for truth.

As Christians, we can hold no other conviction than that scientific truth can only be found if one presupposes and confesses the truth that Christ is the Way, the Truth, and the Life, and that no one can come to the Father—in Whom all things find both their origin and purpose—except through Him. This confession cannot be opposed to science since creation and redemption have the same origin: grace does not destroy nature, but liberates and restores it, and Christ had not come to destroy the works of the Father, but the works of the devil. Confessing Jesus as Christ, therefore, liberates science from the lie and guides it upon the right track. Strictly speaking, the name "Christian science" is not an ideal description for our position. Science as the study of creation is not Christian or un-Christian per se but has truth alone as its standard. That which is true is scientific, even if the whole world were to claim the opposite. And that which is not true is unscientific, even if all the world were to adhere to it. But because there is in science, as everywhere else, so much hypocrisy and falsification, God gave us in His Word a guide and compass, which ought to direct our steps when it comes to scientific research, and which also preserves us from error. Christian science is, therefore, the kind of science that investigates all things in light of Scripture and thereby sees the essence of reality as it truly is. In the eyes of the world, this may be considered foolishness, but the "foolish" God is wiser than mankind and the "weak" God is stronger than man. Our position is never in opposition to, but rather always in accordance with truth.

Index